THE GOOD
LUCK BOOK

THE GOOD LUCK BOOK

ELIZABETH VILLIERS

SENATE

The Good Luck Book

First published in 1923 by T. Werner Laurie Ltd, London

This edition published in 1994 by Senate, an imprint of
Studio Editions Ltd, Princess House, 50 Eastcastle Street,
London W1N 7AP, England

ISBN 1 85958 041 6
Printed and bound in Guernsey by
The Guernsey Press Co Ltd

FOREWORD

In these days of well stocked markets and crowded library shelves, an author has great daring if he or she claims to have written a book which has little or no resemblance to any other.

Yet I make that claim, for surely this Mascot Book treats of its subject in a manner which has not been touched before.

Its inception came from a few words spoken by a gentleman lately returned from the East.

"I don't know that I should call myself superstitious," he said, "but what I have seen in India has convinced me certain inanimate objects have the power of bringing good fortune, while others have an evil influence. . . . There must be an underlying truth in every superstition."

The subject had fascinated me for a considerable time, already I had done a good deal of reading in that direction, and I agreed with him strongly. But after hearing his views I set out to buy some book that would give the history of the best known mascots and the reasons why they are considered fortunate.

I visited a great number of booksellers, I consulted library catalogues, and delved into the treasures of the enchanted shelves at the British Museum and the Guildhall, only to be convinced that the exact book I sought did not exist.

Volumes concerning various means of foretelling the future are plentiful, but were discarded as being wide of the mark. Astrological works were there also, and were much nearer what I wanted, but all are written in a language difficult for all except close students to follow. An enormous number of deeply learned works touch on the subject—histories of peoples and their religions—impressive tomes on Ethnology and Astronomy—fascinating anthologies of Fable and Folklore—these told me of mascots indeed, but the information was hidden away, if the term may be used. It had to be dug out from amidst an enormous amount of other matter.

The more I searched the greater grew the fascination of the subject. I was convinced others would be as interested as I was, and so came the determination that I would collect as comprehensive a list as possible of everyday mascots, and trace the historical or legendary reasons for the beliefs with which they are associated.

Here is the result of my research—a book that deals with mascots, with fortune telling, with "lucky" charms, and colours, and numbers—but which gives also anecdotes of ancient peoples, stories of old religions, history, mythology, and folklore, so that its pages should interest the agnostic and the frank unbeliever as well as those who have faith in the occult.

An enormous amount of research has been necessary. Often the most eminent authorities differ flatly on some particular point, when further investigations have had to be made to explain the divergence, and in other instances great care had to be taken to winnow the wheat from the chaff. As a case in point : A friend gave me a little bronze figure that I am sure is a real mascot because it brought its giver's loving thoughts. The figure was said by its vendor to represent a certain Hindu goddess of good fortune, and I was horrified at my ignorance in not having heard of that particular deity until I consulted an authority at the British Museum and discovered he had not heard of her either ! My little image is a true mascot of Hindu origin, but her name had been bestowed upon her by an enterprising trades-man who had exercised his imagination to advertise his wares.

In all my work I have had the greatest assistance from the Keepers of different departments in the British Museum, and the Librarians both there and at the Guildhall—to the latter I am specially grateful for the trouble they took in finding a collection of seventeenth century almanacks. Also my gratitude is due to Mr W. T. Pavitt, author of the scholarly "Book of Talismans," and his publishers, Messrs Rider & Son, for permission to reproduce ten of his drawings.

But from everyone approached in connection with this book I have received unfailing courtesy and help, so that surely never has any work been begun, carried on, and completed amid more pleasant association. Because of that, by every rule of the occult, it should prove a mascot book indeed to everyone concerned in its production, as well as to each and all of those into whose hands it will fall now that it is in print.

With all my heart I hope it will do so.

ELIZABETH VILLIERS.

THE ORIGIN OF MASCOTS

How Mascots Bring Good Fortune

The word Mascot is a modern introduction into our language, meaning a bringer of good luck, and in that sense it is used here to include amulets, talismans, and charms.

The rules governing the beliefs in the powers of these luck bringers were laid down when the world was young, and in nearly every instance these rules contain some great and lofty thought.

No mascot bought for one's own use or which has been obtained unjustly, can be a bringer of good fortune —indeed it may have exactly the opposite effect. In order to endow its possessor with happiness or health the mascot must come as the gift of a friend—the concrete representation of loving thoughts and prayers—as a token of gratitude, or the reward of some good deed. Seen in this light even the most crude possesses dignity and beauty.

No mascot will bring good fortune to one who is unworthy of it. This rule is not specially laid down in all cases, but, in many, a strong point is made, so that where it is not definitely stated we may take it to be understood.

A knowledge of electricity is suggested by the very ancient rule that no mascot must be allowed to touch the ground. It it falls inadvertently its virtue will be lost, for a time at least.

Mascots are the more powerful if they are worn on the left side in most cases, but to this there are many exceptions.

1

The Influence of Colour

There is the wide spread belief—knowledge would be a better word—that certain colours are lucky or unlucky to certain individuals, or rather that they are harmonious or inharmonious as the case may be.

The belief in this influence of colour is no wild superstition; it is founded on that knowledge of the vibrations of light which in recent times has given birth to the theory that colour and sound are so closely related the one can be actually conveyed by the other. A musician has advertised he teaches his pupils to play the piano by means of " a colour chart "; Whistler called his pictures by musical terms, as his " Nocturne in Blue," to describe their colour schemes; and all are familiar with the expressive slang which declares this or that colour is " loud " or that it " shouts at you."

Astrologically each of the planets as well as each sign of the Zodiac has a particular colour assigned to it, and that colour is harmonious to those born under the influence of the planet or sign. That is fairly easy to understand, but save in a few instances we have no means of knowing the course of reasoning by which the colours were originally assigned. Even by the naked eye we know the planet Mars shines with a red light, hence it is plain why the planet Mars should be given red, and the sign of Aries, of which Mars is the ruling planet, should have red and white. Again, Jupiter, being the most magnificent of the planets, may well have had royal purple given him as tribute to his majesty, but the assignment of other colours is less easy to trace. We can only accept the statements as they have come to us, recognising that they are fragments of the wisdom of other times, and put them to practical test by comparing them with our own knowledge and experience.

It is absolutely certain that every individual has an inborn dislike towards certain colours and a leaning towards others.

Some people are most at home in gaily furnished rooms, others prefer dark hangings, oak panelling or rows of books in sombre bindings along the walls, and each class is more contented, therefore more happy, more healthy, better able to do good work and to enjoy life, when in the surroundings that are harmonious, though exactly why some colours should be discordant to one set of people and the reverse to others we have no means of knowing—yet.

Colour as a Healer

Astrologically it is taught colours have power over disease, that each ill to which flesh is heir is influenced by the planet to which the colour belongs. All this was mapped out with the greatest care, and astrological reasons could be given for each statement. Then the world learnt to sneer at the old beliefs. Fifty years ago medical science was particularly sarcastic at the expense of the " old wives " who said scarlet flannel bound round the loins would cure lumbago when white flannel failed, and no one believed the colours prevailing in a sick room could have the slightest effect on the patient. Yet even then it was admitted green is soothing to the sight, though few remembered the ancients had taught green is the colour of Cancer and that those born under the influence of that particular sign are particularly liable to defects of vision.

Within the last half century opinion has changed again. To-day no medical man of standing will deny that colour does play an important part in healing, and that it is particularly useful in cases of nerve troubles and insanity.

Here, then, is absolute proof that colour influence is an actual and scientific fact, indeed the more the subject is studied the farther removed from fantasy it becomes. And if that is allowed, it opens the door to a clearer understanding of other vibrations, other influences, which being more occult are less easy for us to understand and yet whose existence cannot be denied.

The Influence of Jewels

As in the case of colour, the belief in the power of jewels as mascots is founded on the knowledge of the vibrations of light.

Any jewel mascot must be the jewel itself, not a glass imitation, and though in this instance again our knowledge is not sufficient to state how the particular influence was arrived at, in many cases the old teachings have been absolutely confirmed by modern medical knowledge. Particularly this is so with amber and the amethyst.

The Wonders of Numbers

Very early in the story of the world's religions, sages and students realised few of the daily miracles around us are more marvellous than the absolute exactness of what we call numbers. The multiplication table is a miracle, though it is so familiar most people do not recognise its wonder, and when further studies are made, greater marvels are met.

Those early students searched for proofs which connected these wondrous signs with one or other of the gods, till gradually they had apportioned the all-important figures to various deities. On these researches were founded the belief that certain numbers are fortunate or the reverse to certain people, or rather that numbers, having no power in themselves, yet represent influences which affect all who come within their radius.

There is no such thing as a number which is universally fortunate or the reverse. Each person has his or her individual number decided by the planet ruling at the hour of birth, and what is an absolute bringer of ill to one will be the giver of blessings to another.

As a very familiar example the number 13 may be mentioned.

Of this the digit—the number reached by adding the separate figures together—is 4, one of the numbers given to the Sun. When the Fathers of the Early Church were combating the older faiths, they were careful to point out that everything taught by their predecessors was wrong. Sun-worshippers, in one form or another, were numerous, thus a special attack was made on them and 4 was declared unlucky because it was concerned with Sun worship.

The belief has clung throughout the ages, yet there are plenty of people to whom 4—and therefore 13—is particularly fortunate.

BLACK SPIRITS AND WHITE

Originally all mascots had a religious significance; they were not worn for their own powers but in the hope they might attract the spiritual influences beneficial to their wearers, or at least would repel or combat evil. From the earliest dawn of man's intelligence he has believed that round him the forces of Good and Ill fight a constant battle, and it is in this universal faith can be found the reason why mascots have been credited with power.

From the beginning man has argued that those warring forces of Light and Darkness were each led by One Who is a distinct Individual, commanding the countless forces of lesser powers who fight under His banner. In ancient Egypt they told of the struggles of Osiris the Sun, against Typhon, who was darkness: in Norse mythology, Baldr the white god was killed by Utgarde in alliance with Hotner who was blind—therefore in perpetual darkness. The legends of Greece and Rome were a confused tangle of stories in which gods and demi-gods warred with each other, and in Hebrew and Christian writings the idea is the same.

In the Talmud, Asmodeus the Destroyer was the prince of the demons who drove King Solomon from his throne, till the wise king regained his power by the help of his genii—in the Old Testament (Zachariah III. 1) the High Priest is described as " Standing between the angel of the Lord and Satan," the latter being there to " resist the angel." In the New Testament (Matt. XXV. 41) there is mention of " the devil and all his angels," and in the Book of Revelation (XII. 7) we read :—" There was war in heaven : Michael and his angels fought against the dragon : and the dragon fought, and his angels."

In the Book of Nicodemus, one of the books of the Apocryphal New Testament, there is a still more vivid description of the war between good and evil.

Thus we get the universal acceptance of the existence of two great powers, each with many followers, and from that foundation spread the beliefs in gods and demi-gods; in the genii of Eastern legend; in the familiars of mediæval wizards; in the gnomes and brownies; the elves and little people of folk lore; in the good and bad fairies who attend the christenings of the beautiful princesses in the nursery tales; in the guardian angels of whom we speak so readily; in the guides of the spiritualist—in the Saints of the Church.

How Mascots Gain Their Power

Originally the word "influence" was used astrologically and referred only to the occult power, the virtue, which was believed to flow from the planets to affect all things on earth. Thus the word is used it its strictest sense if we say that mascots have no power of their own, but serve to attract the influence of the Unknown and thus they benefit mankind.

Mascots in Ancient Egypt

The earliest religion of which we have any definite knowledge is that of Ancient Egypt, where men worshipped the Trinity of Osiris (the Father), Isis (the mother) and Horus (the Son). From this creed, beautiful in its inception, proceeded Phallic worship—a word which conveys little to the modern mind save that which is obscene. To the ancient people it suggested nothing impure. In their simplicity, the miracle of pro-creation, of conception, of birth, was the visible sign of God's greatness, and as such was to be worshipped in all purity. Later the religion degenerated into unholy rites, but at the beginning it was the simple faith of a simple people, grasping reverently at the mystery which is a mystery still.

Osiris, King of Heaven, the Universal Father, was represented by the bull on his earthly side, though he was Ra, the sun in its glory, the Giver of Light as well. Isis was the Moon, but had the cow for her earthly symbol, while Horus, the Son, was god of the rising sun, of the newly given light. Remembering this we can understand how symbols of the sun, of the bull, of cow or the crescent moon, all became "mascots" because they were outward signs of the beneficence of the deities they represented.

Of all the Trinity, Isis was the most universally reverenced, to her was given love instead of fear. She was the benefactress of weak and helpless creatures, she guarded every living thing, while the spirits of the dead lay safe in her mother arms.

She was the incarnation of love and wisdom—the ideal mother—and on the floor of her temples was written :—

> " I am everything which hath been, which is and which shall be. Nor hath any mortal pierced my veil."

Far and wide her worship spread, becoming debased or uplifted according to the trend of those who taught, but, as always, amidst the tangle of conflicting creeds and doctrines and theories, a single thread of the original faith remained.

She was Ashtaroth, Astarte, Diana and Hecate in different lands and in different eras, but always the patroness of Sacred Mystery and the protectress of mothers and their offspring.

Osiris, the Sun God, has been identified with the Baal of the Bible, with Jupiter, with the Norse Thor. He waged perpetual warfare with Typhon, the spirit of darkness, and some of the legends are but poetical descriptions of the coming of night and the rising of the sun at morn. The same meaning underlies much that is said of Horus, who was thrust into the darkness of the grave by Typhon, but rose again by means of the ladder which his father let down to save him.

HINDU MASCOTS

Hindu mascots all have reference to the two great religions which hold the East—and have Brahma or Buddha for their Great Spirits.

In one meaning of the word Brahma, no personal deity is described. It stands for a spirit, for " that which is invisible, unsizable, without origin, without either eye or ear, eternal, manifold, all-pervading, undecaying," but in the other sense Brahma is the First Person of the Hindu Trinity, of whom the others are Vishnu, the Preserver, and Siva, the Destroyer. The similarity of thought with that of the Egyptian Trinity is plain.

On the contrary, Buddha is the name of the Great

Teacher, at once Human and Divine, who founded the religion which bears his name about five hundred years before our Christian era. To-day that is the acknowledged faith of hundreds of thousands throughout India, Ceylon, China, Japan, and Thibet.

Practically everything mentioned in connection with Buddha is a talisman, especially his Eight Glorious Emblems (the Wheel of the Law, the Golden Fish, the Conch Shell, the Lucky Diagram, the Lotus, the Umbrella, the Vase, and the Trumpet of Victory.) The Wheel of Life, with which he illustrated his teachings, is a talisman also and so are charms made to represent the print of his feet. All these are dealt with under their separate headings.

Norse Mythology

In Norse mythology we meet another version of the story of Horus who passed into darkness and rose again to be the dawn.

Baldr, the white god, the best beloved son of Odin, inspired all men to love truth and beauty. We are told that " His face shone with splendour, that his brow was called the sun, that he was gentle and good in all things, though brave when the need of battle arose."

His wife, Nanna, was worthy of him. Born a mortal, she was so pure in thought she was permitted to live in both worlds, and as the ideal of perfect womanhood she acted as intermediary between the gods and man.

When Baldr died, killed by the treachery of Utgarde Loki, Odin was so moved by the tears of Nanna that he lessened the power of the goddess of the dead and decreed henceforward Baldr should remain in the place of shades only six months each year, spending the other six in Valhalla with his devoted wife.

Here again is the story of the rising and setting of the sun, told in a way that would be easily understood by the dwellers in those northern latitudes with their many months of night. At the end of their summer—the summer of the midnight sun—Baldr passed into the darkness, to wait till the crowing of the cock woke the goddess of spring, Jostra (or Eostra, from whose name we get our word Easter) caused the earth to wake from her winter sleep.

THE MASCOTS OF THE MIDDLE AGES

In the Middle Ages the practice of white or black magic—that is of rites to propitiate good spirits or evil— was a matter of grave legislation and the magic which might be allowed was carefully defined from that which was forbidden. In connection with these laws, a study was made of mascots whose powers were carefully dis- cussed and universally acknowledged, and reminders of these laws are on every hand still.

In the regalia of the King, in the sacred vessels of the Church, in many customs of our every day life we find traces of these deliberations.

The bishop wore the amethyst, the stone of blessing, on his episcopal ring, as his amulet; while the knightly champion rode into the lists with his mascot on his helm. If that mascot happened to be the favour of his lady so much the greater its power. Then it became the repre- sentation of her loving thoughts and we may be sure she had chosen it with due regard to its astrological value.

THE MASCOTS OF TO-DAY

It is foolish to declare that the belief in mascots belongs to another age, that our own has left it behind. Men may profess to scoff but in daily practice they contradict their words.

The mascot is everywhere to-day, never has it been more popular, as a bishop declared recently when he ful- minated against it in the pulpit.

The airman carries his luck bringer in his " 'bus " when he attempts his greatest flights; the motorist has a mascot on his car. Tennis players, even the most cele- brated champions, go to the courts thus protected, so boxers enter the ring. Cricketers and footballers go to the ground with their mascots, while the thousands of spectators who watch the matches carry the chosen luck- bringers of their favourites, hoping to give them victory. In racing it is the same, and it is well known that of all men gamblers have the greatest belief in luck bringers.

May it not be suggested that the reason is because they study the subject more deeply than most people?

In every country, under every possible circumstance, the belief in the mascot appears.

The lover places his ring—a mascot—on his sweetheart's finger; the bride goes to the altar carrying her mascot of white flowers; the mother buys her baby the coral and bells which are the mascots of childhood.

The business man has a paper-weight on his desk, and its shape is that of a horseshoe or a stag or an elephant—all-important mascots to bring commercial success. Recently an explorer set sail after having been presented with so many mascots by his admirers that he was obliged to leave most of them behind, while a man tried for his life at the Old Bailey, stood in the dock with a row of mascots before him.

It is the same through every class of society. Often the mascot is used unconsciously, but the belief in it is there—it is inborn.

MASCOTS AND THEIR MEANINGS

ABRACADABRA

A " Sigil " or mystic word which would protect from all evil if written on a strip of parchment or paper and worn round the neck. The usual plan was to wear the talisman for nine days, then throw it over the left shoulder, preferably into a running stream.

The actual meaning of the charm has been traced to three Hebrew words, " Pronounce the Blessing," and it is important that the letters should be written in one of the two ways in which they form an inverted triangle.

```
ABRACADABRA
ABRACADABR
ABRACADAB
ABRACADA
ABRACAD
ABRACA
ABRAC
ABRA
ABR
AB
A
```

The other form is :—

```
ABRACADABRA
BRACADABR
RACADAB
ACADA
CAD
A
```

ABRAXAS STONES

ABRAXAS STONE *

Worn to avert the power of evil and to attract all good fortune.

These stones, which were extremely popular as talismans in the Middle Ages, received their name from having the word "abraxas" engraved upon them in Greek letters. The word represents the number 365, and as the Gnostics taught three hundred and sixty-five Spirits emanate from the Supreme Deity, the abraxas stone stood for every virtue and saintly attribute as well as for worldly success. The word almost invariably appears on these stones, accompanied with one or more cabalistic figures. The most usual of these is a strange device of a creature with the head of a cock (to represent watchfulness); the body of a man with the Whip of Power in one hand and the Shield of Wisdom on the other arm; while the legs are formed by two serpents to symbolise the Inner Sense and the Understanding.

The Gnostics were a religious sect, which became very powerful about the time of the Christian era. They incorporated many of the teachings of Buddha, of the Jewish Talmud, and the religion of ancient Egypt in their creed, but afterwards became practically absorbed in the Early Christian Church, though later the Christian fathers sternly denounced the Gnostic teachings.

A belief in the power of talismans and sigils was a definite part of the Gnostic teachings. In the Middle Ages when Gnosticism had practically ceased, their talismans remained and were copied and imitated so that abraxas stones—for the most part forgeries—are common in museums and collections.

* Reprinted by kind permission of William Rider & Son, Ltd., from the "Book of Talismans," by W. T. and K. Pavitt.

ACORN

The acorn is the symbol of Immortality, of Life spring-ing from the earth.

To carry an acorn is to keep off illness and to ensure a long life; it is particularly powerful in guarding its wearer against cholera, a fact which is remarkable seeing that in many country places a ground acorn, mixed with milk, is esteemed as a certain cure for many stomach troubles. As a charm the acorn will bring back an absent lover to the sweetheart he has deserted, gipsies say.

In this case the girl must gather a bit of oak with an acorn on it and a sprig of ash with the "keys." These she lays under her pillow for three nights running, the while she repeats :—

> Acorn cup and ashen key,
> Bid my true love come to me—
> Between moonlight and firelight,
> Bring him over the hills to-night;
> Over the meadows, over the moor,
> Over the rivers, over the sea,
> Over the threshold and in at the door,
> > Acorn cup and ashen key,
> > Bring my true love back to me.

AGATE

A bringer of all good fortune, but above all else the mascot of the tiller of the soil. It belongs to Gemini, and is particularly powerful to those born under that sign.

The belief in the power of an agate as a mascot is world-wide. Not long ago the writer was talking to a gipsy woman who was in high spirits because she had picked up a moss agate on the roadside, so was sure good fortune would follow.

In ancient Rome it was the most fortunate of all stones if mounted in a ring. Whoever wore it on his hand would find favour with the gods, though it was specially the mascot of the farmer or the gardener. Let the agate be tied to the plough and the field would bear a plenteous crop, let the gardener wear an agate on his hand and the ground would yield as it had never done before.

The people of the East, notably of Persia, believe that the agate will confer eloquence and bring good fortune by way of inheritance or through a will or other document. In addition it will show where any hidden treasure is buried, and it will make its wearer lovable and beloved.

It is hardly necessary to add that the agate is a favourite stone for a man's signet ring—a fashion that is directly traceable to these beliefs.

Nor do its powers end as a luck bringer.

Finely powdered and mixed with wine it should be drunk as an antidote to the bite of a snake, while if the same mixture is used as an external lotion and tied over a poisoned wound, healing will follow.

The Mohammedans mix powdered agate with apple juice as a remedy for delirium or insanity, and say that to carry an agate will shield from the infection of fever. The Romans taught that an agate would cure all affections of the eye.

There are many kinds of agate commonly distinguished as the moss, the eye, the onyx, the iris, the white and the ribbon, though sometimes the moss agate is called the tree agate and the iris the rainbow. These names are easy to understand—the one stone has delicate black markings which bear a fanciful resemblance to the branches of a tree or to certain growths of moss, while the other is crossed by bands of colour in a not-unrainbow-like style.

Often in its natural state the agate appears as a milky white stone, when it is artificially coloured for commercial purposes as it takes dyes readily. Thus agates of the most brilliant colours are on sale, notably those of vivid green.

AGLA

See Sigil.

AGNUS DEI

A sacred emblem, dating from early Christian times. It represents a Lamb carrying a flag and cross, and was treasured as an amulet protecting from accidents, storm or infection.

AMBER

People born under Leo should wear amber constantly, but it is absolutely unlucky to those of Taurus.

This beautiful " stone " dates from the far-back time when man was not, and the face of the earth was clothed by mighty trees and growths for which we have no name, though outline of trunk and branch and leaf can be traced in our coal fields by those who can read the signs aright.

And amber is the fossilised remains of a plant which grew amid the trees that are our coal.

So beautiful is amber, so filled with strange properties, there is little wonder it has been venerated from mankind's earliest days, or that many legends have been woven round it.

To begin with, it is highly charged with that mystery we call electricity—the force we all know and yet of which we know nothing.

It was because amber emitted sparks of fire when rubbed that, under like circumstances, it had power to attract and hold certain small objects as a magnet, men first realised the existence of some strange power.

Experiments were held with amber, the existence of electricity was brought to light, and to the power the name of the stone was given. For in Greek amber is called " elektron," and from " elektron " came our word " electricity."

One of the oldest theories of the origin of amber was that it was formed by the direct heat of the sun focussed on the earth, hence, perhaps, it came that it was dedicated to the sun.

Amber is one of the most ancient of mascots. Beads made of it have been found in the oldest of the Egyptian tombs, and amongst the tributes Cæsar exacted from Britain was the payment of a certain amount of amber every year.

Apart from its occult powers it was credited with high medicinal virtues, and was said to prevent the spread of infection if held in the mouth—for which reason the men of the East had the mouthpieces of their pipes made of it. The custom spread to the West and obtains amongst us still.

The Chinese burn amber as incense, so do the Mohammedans; and a necklace of amber protects its wearer from all forms of witchcraft and ill-wishing—providing the birthdate is favourable.

Wearing such a necklace would do more than that. Medicinally it was a cure for erysipelas and goitre, while deafness, indigestion and loss of teeth are amongst the other troubles from which it protects its wearer.

So said the ancients : later medical science laughed at the teachings, and now—

Quite recently a great authority announced that a string of amber beads worn constantly round the throat will strengthen it and banish danger from many of the diseases liable to attack that particular part—as goitre. His theory is that amber being so highly charged with electricity, the beads set up an electric circle by their contact with the warmth of the body, thus bringing into existence a protective power of which it is impossible to speak too highly.

Again—in the old days it was said a baby should wear amber to save it from fits while teething. To-day a volatile oil extracted from amber is used medicinally in cases of infantile convulsions.

AMETHYST

The birth stone of Pisces people, but a mascot for all.

" The beneficent stone," as it was called by the ancients, is fortunate for lovers and for business men, sportsmen and hunters. It calms fears, it cures many diseases, particularly neuralgia and nerve troubles, and is the great talisman against drunkenness.

How ancient this latter idea may be we do not know, but it is far, far beyond anything we can count. The ancient Egyptians wore the stone for that purpose, so did the Greeks, while Aristotle tells a legend to account for its power.

According to him Amethyst was the name of a beautiful nymphe who had the ill-fortune to attract the admiration of Bacchus during one of his drunken orgies. The god pursued her, and horrified at the thought of such a lover, she prayed to Diana, goddess of chastity, that she might be saved.

The goddess heard her prayer, for as Bacchus seized her, Amethyst was changed to a gleaming jewel in his hand. Apparently he was sobered by the surprise, and being somewhat ashamed of himself, endowed the jewel with the rich purple tint of his favourite wine. At the same time he ordained that in memory of his love and her chastity, Amethyst should have power to weaken his influence over his worshippers and to save them from the degradation to which he would drag them.

Throughout the ages the amethyst has been called the Beneficent Stone—the Stone of Love—the Stone of Healing—the Stone of Peace—the only mascot which is fortunate to all and has no ill effects on any.

More than any other jewel it is used for episcopal rings.

Uplifted on the hands of bishops, amethysts have sent an influence of holiness and peace over countless kneeling flocks. Rosaries for use in special times of war or pestilence were made from it in the Middle Ages, since those who prayed as they held the stone were more easily led into a state of tranquility and calm.

Those rosaries are specially interesting, for in ancient Egypt the amethyst was valued as the stone to calm fears, while Pliny tells us that if the symbols of the sun and moon are engraved upon an amethyst it becomes the most sustaining of all jewels. As a sequel to this, modern medical science has discovered that the purple rays of the amethyst exercise a calming influence over hysterical patients, and many cases of acute neuralgia and other nervous troubles, which have defied ordinary treatment, have been absolutely cured when an amethyst has been drawn lightly to and fro over the patient's forehead.

In declaring that the amethyst is the stone sacred to lovers, tradition adds that Saint Valentine wore one constantly—which is likely enough since he was a bishop of the Christian Church, so probably had an amethyst in his episcopal ring. Partly because of its associations with him, but far more because of the elder traditions concerning it, the stone is the most fortunate of all gifts to pass between sweethearts.

ANANIZAPTA

See Sigil.

ANCHOR

The sign of hope, the promise of a safe return, therefore the favourite mascot for sailors or all who are going journeys by land or sea.

ANDROMEDA

Statuettes of this Greek princess were used in ancient Rome to promote successful love affairs or to ensure happy married life.

In mythology Andromeda was the daughter of the King of Etheopia, whose country was ravaged by a sea monster. To save the land, her sacrifice was demanded, she was bound naked to a rock and left to the mercy of the terrrible foe, but the hero Perseus flew to her rescue, changed the monster into a stone, set the princess free, and married her.

ANGELS

A bringer of blessings—a bearer of good tidings—are what is meant by the word angel, and the names of the seven archangels written on slips of paper form a very powerful mascot.

The connection of these messengers of good with astrology is very ancient. In the Hebrew sacred books it is taught that in addition to the seven archangels there are twelve massaloth—that is Signs of the Zodiac—each " with thirty chiefs of armies attendant on it, while each chief has thirty legions consisting of thirty leaders, each with thirty captains under him, each captain with thirty men "—a definite use of the mystic 3—and " all these are the ministering spirits of Israel."

The astrologers adopted the Jewish belief in these angels and assigned the seven chief spirits by name to various planets, thus :—Zaphiel rules Saturn ; Zadkiel, Jupiter ; Camel, Mars ; Raphael, the Sun ; Haniel, Venus ; Michael, Mercury ; Gabriel, the Moon.

These seven names written in red have special power to promote holiness and dispel evil thoughts.

ANGLES

Talismans in the familiar shapes of the capital letters L or A were symbols of the god Thoth, and were worn to promote wisdom and knowledge and justice. They helped the Law Giver in his judgments, the student at his study. See also Solomon's Seal.

ANKH

An Egyptian talisman made in the form of a cross crowned by a ring. It is worn to bring prosperity, and to increase knowledge.

APHRODITE

The Greek goddess of Love, who was Venus in Rome, and Hathor in Egypt. Mascots in her likeness bestowed on their owners the power to charm, and induced happy love.

The sparrow, the dove, the swan, the rose, the myrtle, and the poppy were all sacred to Aphrodite, who was a very gentle goddess in her earlier form, to whom only fruit and flowers might be offered. Later her worship became brutalised, and sensual orgies took the place of the poetic rites which had been held in her honour previously.

APIS

See Bull.

AQUAMARINE

The mascot of happy marriage, therefore the ideal gift for a bridegroom to give his bride on their wedding day. It is fortunate to sweethearts also, as it ensures constancy, and is a powerful mascot for sailors. As a birthstone it belongs to Scorpio and is fortunate also to the people of Aries, though in a lesser degree.

The aquamarine is the same stone as the beryl except for colour, but while the true beryl is either white or blue, the aquamarine has the bluish green tint of the sea—hence its name.

In the Middle Ages it was credited with high medicinal value in troubles of the throat and jaws. Necklaces made of it were worn as cures for toothache, and it was recommended as a preventative of stomach or liver troubles.

ARIES

See Zodiac.

ARROW HEAD

A love charm to secure the winning of affection from the one beloved, also a powerful protector from the evil eye.

The first arrow heads were flints, laboriously chipped into triangular shape, and when their actual use had been forgotten, other races found those arrow heads and believed they had been made by fairy workmen, or at least came from some supernatural source. Lang says :—

" After the heavy rain of a thunderstorm has washed the soil, it sometimes happens that a child or a rustic finds a wedgeshaped piece of metal or a few triangular flints in a field or near a road. There were no such pieces of metal, there were no such flints, lying there yesterday. and the finder is puzzled about the origin of the objects on which he has lighted. He carries them home and the village wisdom determines that the wedge-shaped piece of metal is a ' thunderbolt,' or that the bits of flint are ' elf shots ' or the heads of fairy arrows. Such things are still treasured in remote nooks of England, and the ' thunderbolt' is applied to cure certain maladies by the touch."

Those flint arrow heads are dipped in water and the water drunk by women suffering from feminine ailments, while the flints themselves are worn round the neck as protection from the Evil Eye or from infection.

The arrow, as apart from the arrow head, is a talisman for lovers from it connection with Cupid, and the familiar device of the arrow or dart which pierces two hearts and thus binds them together. It forms a lovers' charm to secure that the thoughts of the absent remain true.

ARTEMESIA

An important Chinese mascot is the artemesia, or sweet flag of which a leaf is nailed on either side of the chief entrance to a house, ensuring good fortune for those within. It is imporant, however, that the leaves should be placed in position on the morning of the fifth moon of the year.

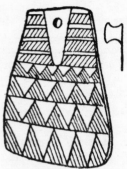

PREHISTORIC AXE HEAD *

AXE

The sign of power, the giver of success.

The axe was venerated as a totem amongst the very earliest races of which we have knowledge, and in the remains of the Stone Age are many talismans carved to represent axe heads and pierced so they could be worn on cords round the neck. The sword of State which is carried before the King on all ceremonial occasions is a direct descendant of the prehistoric axe as a symbol of power.

BACCHUS

The god of revelry, see Amethyst. Masks of Bacchus were talismans hung on fruit trees to secure good crops and worn as protection from the evil eye.

BADGER

One of the animal's teeth is a gambler's mascot. This should be sewn in the right-hand pocket of the waistcoat to ensure good fortune when playing cards.

BAMBOO

The bamboo with seven knots appears in a well known Hindu talisman, that gives wisdom and power.

The talisman is a circle engraved with triangles, and across the circle, forming the spokes of the wheel, as it were, lie the seven-

BAMBOO WITH SEVEN KNOTS *

* Reprinted by kind permission of William Rider & Son, Ltd., from the "Book of Talismans," by W. T. and K. Pavitt.

knotted bamboo and a serpent. Every part of the device has a mystic significance. The circle is the symbol of Eternity, the triangles stand for the Hindu Trinity (Brahma the Creator, Vishnu the Preserver, Siva the Destroyer), the Serpent for wisdom, and the bamboo for the seven degrees of learning the devout must possess.

BANGLE

Another form of the ring (which see) a symbol of eternity.

In another sense the bangle is a sign of possession. When a girl slips a " slave bangle " on her arm, it is a symbol that she belongs to the giver, and will not break the bond until Eternity.

BAT

In the East, bat talismans are worn to promote longevity. Sometimes the talisman is in the form of five bats linked together, when they stand for " That Which All Men Desire," viz., Luck, Wealth, Longevity, Health and Peace. Another form of the same mascot is two bats, which represent good wishes. This is a favourite gift between friends.

The bat is mentioned in charms and incantations all over Britain, but nothing very definite seems known of it. In some parts of the country, in Berkshire, for instance, country boys repeat a queer doggerel on seeing a bat :—

> Bat, bat, come under my hat,
> And I'll give you a slice of bacon.

No explanation is forthcoming for what seems an inane rhyme, but it may be that the words, so meaningless now, bear a phonetic resemblance to other words in a forgotten language that repeated a spell to change the bat from a harbinger of evil to the bringer of good luck. This suggestion may not seem utterly wild when it is remembered that the " eina, dena, dina, dess," with which children in their games decide who shall be " he," is believed to be the last fragment of the Druidical language, the very incantation with which the priests of the groves chose amid their captives the human sacrifice who was to meet his death upon the altar stone.

BAY

See Laurel.

BEADS

Beads have the power of bestowing various good gifts on their wearers, the particular type of fortune depending on the kind of beads worn and the birth date of the person wearing them. Details will be found under the names of various stones and jewels.

The wearing of beads as talismans is very ancient, and in the East strings of beads are placed in bales of goods to save them from thieves. All over the world children are given bead necklaces—chiefly of coral—to protect them from the Evil Eye, and though the "telling of the beads," which forms part of the religious ceremony of more than one creed, was latterly adopted as a method of refreshing the memory and thus keeping the succession of prayers in the right order, originally beads were used in worship from the belief they held occult power.

Glass beads have been found in very ancient tombs, and there is a tradition that the Druids had a Magic Egg, believed to have been a large glass bead, which they used for divination—it was the forerunner of the globe of the modern crystal-gazers.

BEANS

Drive away evil influences, protect children and promote happiness generally.

"The Lucky Bean" is quite a common charm to find on watch chains and bangles, probably because in the Western Highlands a certain kind of bean is credited with the power to drive away evil spirits and to confer wealth. The oldest Egyptian tombs frequently contain beans, from the idea that as the bean retains the spark of life for an indefinite time it is the emblem of immortality. This belief must have been founded on knowledge, for beans, found in tombs of immense age, have sprouted on being brought into the light—and this after being buried for three of four thousand years.

From this teaching of the Egyptians grew the belief that beans were connected with the dead. The Romans threw beans on the fire to drive away ghosts, and in Scotland necklaces of beans were worn as charms against witches. Martin, in his " Description of the Western Islands of Scotland," tells a story in regard to this :—

" There is a variety of nuts called Mulluka Beans, some of which are used as amulets against witchcraft or an evil eye, particularly the white one. And on this account they are worn about children's necks and if any evil is intended them they say the bean changes into a black colour. That they did change colour I found true from my own observation, but cannot be positive as to the cause of it. Malcolm Campbell, steward of Harries, told me that some weeks before my arrival there all his cows gave blood instead of milk for several days together. One of his neighbours told his wife this must be witchcraft and it would be easy to remove it if she would but take the white bean called the Virgin Mary's nut and lay it in the pail into which she was to milk the cows. This advice she presently followed and having milked one cow into the pail with the nut in it, the milk was all blood and the nut changed its colour to dark brown. She used the nut again and all the cows gave good pure milk which they ascribe to the virtue of the nut. This very nut Mr Campbell presented to me, and I have it still."

CARLINS

The mid Sunday in Lent was called Carlin Sunday from the custom of eating grey peas or beans baked in fat, and well within the last fifty years every cottager in the North Riding of Yorkshire would have her dish of hot carlins on that Sunday morning to offer to everyone who came to the house.

" I'll none have good luck all the year if you none taste my carlins," she would say.

BEANS IN CHRISTMAS PUDDINGS

Beans played a part in old Christmas festivities. Later came the custom of putting coins and thimbles and so forth into the Christmas pies or the Twelfth cakes with the idea that those who receive the portion with the little gift can read from it their fortune for the coming year, but originally it was a bean and a pea alone which were introduced into the Christmas cake, and the person who received the former was elected King of the Revels, while the pea proclaimed the queen. Herrick writes :—

> Now, now the mirth comes
> With a cake full of plums,
> Where bean's the king of sport here,
> Besides we must know
> The pea also
> Must revel as queen of the court here.

Lucky beans will be found on many of the sets of charms which are sold at Christmastide to be stirred into the Christmas pudding that has taken the place of the older cake or pie or porridge.

BEANS AS LOVE CHARMS

Beans had their part in the preparation of love charms.

A very old tradition declares that if a girl wishes to win the love of a man who is cold to her, or to bring about a reconciliation with a lover from whom she is parted, she should place seven beans in a circle on the road along which he will walk and keep watch, herself unseen.

If he strides over the beans, or even if he treads on them, he will come to her and tell her of his love, but if he makes a detour and walks on the other side of the way the charm has failed in its purpose. Apparently there was no reason why the circle of beans need remain in sight, the girl could bury them under a layer of earth or leaves if she wished.

BEAN FEASTS

Most dictionaries give the reason why workmen's outings are called "Bean Feasts" as :—"Perhaps because beans were served there." But with all respect it may be suggested the name comes from a revel, such as that of Twelfth Night presided over by a bean-elected king.

BEANS AS A THREAT

The slang phrase " I'll give him beans " is not so easily explained unless it is a threat to the ghosts and evil spirits which the bean has power to exorcise.

BEAR

The symbol of strength and watchfulness.

Of all the constellations that cluster of stars we call the Great Bear is the best known, and many times the question has been asked why it was given its name for no possible resemblance to a bear can be traced. Yet the name is world-wide. As far back as the time of Homer the Greeks called those stars The Bear, and the North American Indians say the four chief stars in the constellation are the bear, while the little one at the side is the pot in which the hunters would cook him. Andrew Lang quotes Muller who suggests that the name is a mistaken reading of two Sanskrit words meaning " The Bright Ones," and if that is so the name is understandable. Less easy of explanation is the legend which is found the world over in connection with the constellation.

The Greeks described the stars as a princess who was changed by Zeus into the likeness of a bear in which shape she was shot by Artemis, but before that had become the mother of a child, and from that child sprang all the people of Arcadia. Now the Australian aborigines, the Red Indians and the Bedouins all believe they are descended from a woman who was changed into an animal, and all call those stars the Bear.

BEE

A brooch or charm in the shape of a honey bee brings success in business—it is the emblem of perseverance and thrift.

A live bee is a mascot also. If one comes buzzing round be sure you do not hurt it nor drive it away : it is the foreteller of success. That belief seems common all over England, yet in Suffolk they say that if a hive of bees " swarm " in or near your house and is unclaimed by the owner, some misfortune will follow. In many places the custom of " telling the bees " whenever an important event happens in the family is followed, and you will see a scrap of white ribbon fluttering on the hives at the time of a wedding, or a bit of black crape, should there have been a death.

If a humble bee or " dumbledore " enters through your door expect the coming of a stranger, say gipsies.

BEETLE OR SCARAB

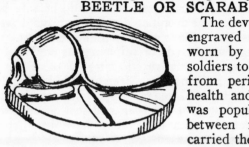

SCARAB

The device of a scarab, engraved on rings was worn by the Egyptian soldiers to preserve them from peril and ensure health and strength. It was popular as a gift between friends as it carried the belief that in presenting a scarab you literally gave good fortune to the recipient.

The original of this rather queer mascot is a small beetle common in Egypt. It has the habit of laying its eggs in clay which it fashions into a neat ball with the eggs in the centre. This done the scarab sets off on its travels rolling the clay ball before it, and often goes a considerable distance before finding the spot where it thinks its eggs can be left to hatch in safety.

In ancient Egypt sages watched this beetle as people watch it to-day, and from its mother-love they evolved a parable. The action of the rolling ball they took to be typical of the movement of the earth, and in the fact that within the ball lay the eggs holding the germ of life, they saw the symbol of Creation, of Regeneration, and Immortality.

Thus the humble scarab came to have a very high and deep significance. It was called the Symbol of the Sun god, Khepera, who creates life, and because it typified the resurrection of the spirit, little figures of scarabs, generally of green stones mounted in gold, were placed in the tombs. The particular scarab shown in the illustration is an engraved stone, now in the British Museum, and shown in the Museum's Illustrated Guide to " The Department of Greek and Roman Antiquities."

BELLS

Powerful talismans against all evil spirits, particularly to protect the young or the weak.

The bell is one of the oldest talismans in the world, and from the dawn of civilization children were placed near bells in the belief that there they would be safe because the gods would be propitiated and evil spirits driven off by the bells—the rattle is a bell in a different form.

Bells or gongs were used for rejoicings as well as for mournful wailing amid the mystic rites of the Phœnecians, and by them bells may have been brought to Britain, but it is certain bells played an important part in the Druidical rites. Indeed it has been said that all over the world, wherever the Sun and Moon have been worshipped, bells have been used.

When the boar was sacrificed to Diana in Rome at the August festival, a sanctus or bell was attached to the victim's neck, and we find bells appearing in countless other mysteries and divinations. Probably to this can be traced the superstition that fortunes may be read in tea cups, for what are cups except inverted bells?

Not only children but soldiers sought the protection of the gods by the ringing of bells. The Greeks fastened bells to the inner part of their shields that they might ring in praise of the gods as they were borne to battle, and when Cæsar landed in Britain he was met by a horde of warriors who carried tinkling bells upon the handles of their spears. The Goths who came from the north to overrun southern Europe, went into battle clanging bells in honour of their gods, and when victory was won they sounded their bells again as token of thanksgiving—as we ring our church bells in the time of rejoicing.

Until quite recent years the Chinese soldiers went to fight, ringing bells; the wind bells hanging from their pagodas are to drive away evil spirits; while their priests and people ring bells at the time of an eclipse just as the natives of Africa beat their tom-toms—again a form of bell.

In brief, the belief that the powers of evil fear bells is world-wide, and has been maintained through countless ages. At first purely religious symbols, bells became worn as personal charms, then with the passing of years the reasons for their use became forgotten, but the bells remained.

Children are given bells because they are pretty toys, bells are hung on the collars of sledge horses, or of " bell teams," and of hansom cab horses—after the introduction of rubber tyres—because they are useful as warnings of approach, but originally all these bells were charms to protect against danger. In the same way the bells of the temples which rang to scare demons remain in church steeples to summon worshippers to prayer.

The passing bell—or the Soul Bell as it is often called —is another instance.

When a human being lay dying his relations gathered round his bed ringing bells to frighten away the fiends who were lurking to snatch the soul as it trembled on Borderland. With the coming of Christianity the Fathers of the Church ordered that a bell should be rung as a warning that all who heard might pause and pray for the departing soul. The fundamental idea remained the same but its execution varied.

For a considerable time the new idea and the old lived on side by side as it were, for Grose tells us :—

" The passing bell was anciently rung for two purposes; one to bespeak the prayers of all good Christians for a soul just departing; the other to drive away the evil spirits who stood at the bed's foot and about the house ready to seize their prey, or at least to molest and terrify the soul in its passage; but by the ringing of that bell (for Durandus informs us evil spirits are much afraid of bells) they are kept aloof; and the soul, like a hunted hare, gained the start, or had what sportsmen called the law. . . . The dislike of spirits to bells is mentioned in the Golden Legend by Wynkyn de Worde."

BENZAIBEN

This deity is the Japanese Apollo, the god of grace and beauty. His portrait is a powerful talisman, banishing evil influences and uplifting the soul.

BERYL

What has been written of the aquamarine holds good for the beryl which has exactly the same attributes astrologically. As a birth stone it belongs to the same period and in the East is a favourite wedding gift, being the emblem of purity.

BES

The Egyptian god of laughter, merry-making, and good luck, as well as the patron of beauty and the guardian angel of children. As a mascot he protects all young things and ensures a happy, harmonious atmosphere in the home.

In ancient Egypt little figures of Bes with his pot belly, his bat's ears, and quaint smile, were very popular, and were worn to dispel clouds of trouble and to bring joy into life. Later on, in Greece and Rome, jolly Bes degenerated into dissolute Bacchus, but in that form had little in common with the original conception.

BETROTHAL

See Love.

BILLIKEN

A very modern mascot, a bringer of general good luck. This queer little chap with his fascinating smile is quite a recent invention, at least under his present name. No search that I have been able to make throws any light upon his origin, and I think it is certain that he had a purely commercial christening.

But whoever first made Billiken and put him on the market to become a popular mascot, drew his idea from the Egyptian deity, Bes (which see).

BIRTH DATES

See under Zodiac for the influence of the birth date on the character. Also for fortunate stones, colours, metals and days.

BISHAMON

The Japanese god whose likeness gives lofty thoughts, drives away despair, and encourages courage and hope. He is the god of Glory, and is shown as carrying a spear in his right hand and a pagoda in his left, the spear representing Power as does the thunderbolt of Jupiter or the hammer of Thor; the pagoda giving inspiration and hope.

BLACK CAT

See Cat.

BLACKTHORN

A mascot for lovers and a charm against " ill wishers."

All over England you will find it said that if a man tells a girl he loves her when they are standing near a blackthorn bush, she may look forward confidently to a happy marriage, while a blackthorn leaf carried in the purse will bring good fortune.

Wishes wished beside the blackthorn will be granted, and a bit of the wood of the bush held in the hand will prevent the power of " ill wishers." Gipsy men carry sticks of blackthorn, as protection from perils lurking in the road.

BLOODSTONE

The mascot for all born under Scorpio or Aries, but should be avoided by Cancer people. Providing the birth-date is right it is the most powerful of all mascots for soldiers.

The bloodstone is a kind of green jasper flecked with red, and as it is a hard stone capable of great polish, its popularity for seals and signet rings is readily under-stood. Its use is very ancient. The Egyptians wore rings set with bloodstones on their thumbs, probably because the thumb is ruled astrologically by the planet Mars, and Mars is the ruling planet of the House of Aries, to which the stone has been assigned.

It is the soldiers' talisman, not only bestowing courage but shielding from danger, while when wounds had been received it was said the stone had power to stop the bleeding. Again modern medical knowledge throws a curious side-light on an old teaching, for to-day an oxide is made from the bloodstone which is used in cases of excessive hæmorrhage.

In some parts of India the natives will render " first aid " to a wounded man by dipping a bloodstone in water and binding it on his hurt.

In an old book written by Thomas Boyle and published

in 1675, entitled " The Origin and Virtue of Gems," there
is the story of a man who suffered from such dreadful
bleeding at the nose that his life was endangered, until
" an ancient gentleman " gave him a bloodstone and bade
him wear it round his neck.   This he did with the result
that the bleeding ceased and, we are told, he performed
another remarkable cure by lending his bloodstone to a
neighbour who was similiarly afflicted.

The bloodstone was credited with other medicinal
virtues in the long past. In ancient Egypt King Nechepsos
wore an engraved bloodstone to cure himself of indigestion; others of the ancients saw in it the amulet of
long life, while in the Middle Ages it became the acknowledged mascot of farmers and breeders of cattle.

BOW
The symbol of hope and of happy love. See Sagittarius,
under Zodiac.

BROOMSTICK
The Hampshire gipsies say that if an " ill wisher " is
approaching the house you may protect yourself by placing a broomstick across the threshold so that a cross is
formed.   The enemy will pass the door or if the house
is entered all power for ill will be destroyed.   The same
idea runs through the belief that if sticks or straws are
laid across each other in the path a witch has to tread her
power to harm will leave her.

BUCKLE OF ISIS
See Cornelian.

BULL
The emblem of dignity, strength and power.

In Ancient Egypt the bull was the sign of Osiris the
Creator, the giver of life, the earthly father, in contrast
to the other Osiris, the giver of light.   In that sense the
bull is the symbol of earthly influences and as such he is
used in astrology (see Taurus) but he is always patient
and plodding and persevering, so is favourable to workers.

In other ancient faiths we find the bull mentioned constantly, always from the same point of view as that with
which he was regarded by the Egyptians.   He was the

symbol of Baal as well as of Osiris, and Jupiter frequently disguised himself in the shape of a bull.

BULL'S HEAD

The Etruscans wore discs of metal engraved with bulls' heads as talismans to give success in love or to secure lasting friendship. In addition these discs ensured good health and length of life.

BULLA

An ancient sign of freedom as well as a talisman worn to avert the evil eye.

The Bulla was a curious locket, either heart-shaped or round, made of gold, and hollow so that it could contain a slip of parchment on which a sigil was written. In Rome the Bulla was the badge of those who were free born. Often the tusk of some animal was attached to it, as a tusk increases the power of any mascot against the evil eye.

BUNS (HOT CROSS)

All sorts of beliefs cluster around Hot Cross Buns, the most persistent being that they never mildew as all other kinds of bread will do, also that if a bun is kept from one year to another there will be no danger of the house being burnt down. The Hot Cross Bun is thus a powerful mascot against fire.

BUSINESS (Mascots to Attract Success in)

Practically all mascots assist in bringing success to business ventures, providing that those ventures are being carried on honourably. For the special luck bringers of traders, however, see : Amethyst, Bee, Bull, Cornucopia, Cricket, Deer, Dragon, Grasshopper, Elephant, Fish, Fox, Hammer, Moonstone, Narita, and Olivine.

BYZANTINE RINGS

See Rings.

CADUCEUS

The Wand of Mercury, the Rod of Healing and of Peace, a powerful mascot healing quarrels, driving away sickness, giving eloquence and youthfulness to its possessor. It was a very mystic talisman, and its influence was all for good.

Apollo gave Mercury a staff surmounted by a pine

cone—symbol of healing—with wings to represent the flight of man's thoughts to the higher things. The god added that whoever carried the rod would have a marvellous gift of speech and would be able to smooth away all quarrels by bending his hearers to his will.

CADUCEUS

Armed with this magic wand, Mercury went forth and presently saw two serpents in deadly fight. He laid his rod between them and exerting his newly bestowed eloquence ended the bitter feud. From that time the serpents were added to the rod; they typify regeneration, that as a serpent casts its skin and emerges in a new and glittering form, so man may rid himself of his lower nature and rise to the heights whither the mystic wings will bear him.

CAMEL

As a mascot typifies a patient friend, one who bears another's burdens with courage and devotion. It brings success after struggles, and is the emblem of sympathy and kind thoughts.

CANCER

See Zodiac.

CAPRICORN

See Zodiac.

CARBUNCLE

The birth stone of those born under Pisces, and as a secondary stone it is fortunate to the people of Aries and Scorpio.

In olden days this was called the Luminous Stone, and many legends were told of its power of retaining and giving forth light—amongst them that a very large carbuncle was taken by Noah into the ark to act as a lamp! That quaint adventurer, Sir John Maunderville, who sailed from England on Michaelmas Day, 1322, for the Far East, tells us that the Grand Cham followed Noah's example :—

" This emperor hath in his chamber in one of the pillars of gold, a carbuncle half a foot long which in the night gives so great a light and shining that it is as light as day."

The Hebrews called the carbuncle the " baaketh " or " lightning stone," the name coming from the Hebrew word for lightning, and Pliny tells us that the deep red carbuncles are masculine while the paler stones are feminine.

To-day, as in ages past, the Arabs have the fixed idea that a carbuncle will protect its wearer from wounds in battle, and the same belief obtains amongst the tribes of northern India. Thus it has become the mascot of soldiers, though during the Middle Ages it protected against plague and infections as well as against wounds. Also it raised spirits, dispelled evil thoughts, reconciled friends who had quarrelled, attracted success in business, and was a very powerful charm against all diseases of the throat and stomach.

CARDS

Playing cards have been called the Devil's Books, and coming to us from the East where they are of remote antiquity, they have been used for spells and divinations through numberless ages. To attempt anything like a detailed description of these would be impossible here, but it may be added an old tradition declares whoever gets the deuce of Clubs will have a run of good luck, while the four of Clubs—sometimes called the Devil's Bedstead—is a sign of misfortune.

Brand, in his " Antiquities," quotes " an old chapbook " as giving the following account of how the future may be read by the drawing of cards blindfold from the pack :

This noble king of diamonds shows
Thou long shalt live where pleasure flows;
But when a woman draws the king,
Great melancholy songs she'll sing.

Now if the Queen of Diamonds fair,
She shows thou shalt some office bear;
O, Woman, if she falls to you,
Friends thou wilt have and not a few.
If now the Knave of Diamonds come,
Be sure beware the martial drum;
Yet if a woman draws the knave,
She shall much better fortune have.
He that draws the ace of hearts
Shall surely be a man of parts;
But she that draws it, I profess,
Will have the curse of idleness.
He who can draw this deuce, shall be
Endowed with generosity;
But when a woman draws this card,
It doth betide her cruel hard.
The man who gets hold of this tray,
Always bound, always obey.
A woman that shall draw this sort,
Will sure drink brandy by the quart.

It is unfortunate—or the reverse—that Brand's quotation breaks off here and gives the meaning of no other cards.

CARP

See Fish.

CAT

All over the world are traditions concerning cats, perhaps the most common being that if any cat—but especially a black one—comes to the house it is a sign of good fortune, so long as the creature is kindly treated. The Chinese alone dislike the advent of a black cat: to them it is a warning of sickness.

According to "Demonology and Devil Lore," by Conway, a three-coloured cat is a certain protection against the house in which it lives being destroyed by fire. The same work adds that a black cat can cure epilepsy (how is not stated), and protects gardens.

In Guernsey they say that to see a black cat passing the window is a sign that a stranger is coming, and in the South of England a black cat is a charm which ensures a husband to the daughter of the house.

If a cat with double claws is found it is the greatest luck bringer of all, and must be most carefully guarded and protected.

In any case, if a cat asks your help and is driven away or otherwise ill-treated, ill luck is sure to follow.

In Ancient Egypt cats were sacred animals associated with the goddess Pakht or Sekhet, as the name is variously rendered, who was portrayed as having the head of a cat. Our word " cat " is a form of the name of the goddess though the Egyptian word for cat was Mau. Osiris disguised himself as a cat at times, which may account for the sacred character given to the animal in Egypt, and for the vague legends of " witches' " cats which belong to Christian times. In the British Museum there is an Egyptian drawing of Ra the Sun god (who was Osiris) " in the form of the Great Cat " cutting off the head of Aapep, the god of darkness and evil.

Later, cats of all sorts, but black cats especially, were called the companions of witches. Thus any injury offered to a cat would bring down the vengeance of its friends, while if it were well treated, the witches—or Sekhet of you prefer the older version—would surely reward its benefactors. If only as lessons of mercy to helpless creatures these old beliefs are worth consideration.

CAT'S EYES

As a birth stone the cat's eye belongs to Cancer, but whatever the birth date it is a powerful mascot against all diseases of the chest or throat. The mere possession of a cat's eye is sufficient to cure a sufferer from asthma, while if the stone is tied round the neck of a child there will be no fear of the discomfort and danger of croup.

It has a soothing effect on excitable or nervous patients, and is beneficial in cases of mental disorders.

In India it is one of the most valued of mascots for there the belief obtains that whoever owns a cat's eye will never find his fortune grow less, while apart from all else it is the gambler's mascot, bringing luck in all games of chance.

It is a very beautiful stone of the chrysoberyl family, usually milky white in colour though yellow specimens are not uncommon, and others are tinted brown or red.

CAUL

There is a very ancient belief that any child born with a caul—that it with a detachable hood-like skin covering the head and face at birth—will be extremely fortunate through life, as a caul is the most powerful luck bringer in the world.

Unlike most mascots the caul has power for good even when it is obtained by purchase, and midwives used to do a brisk trade in cauls, selling them to sailors or travellers about to undertake long voyages, since the possessor of a caul could never be drowned, or to lawyers and politicians because the caul gave eloquence and persuasive speech. During the seventeenth century advertisements offering cauls for sale were quite common in the newspapers, the prices asked varying from ten to thirty pounds. Less that a year ago at least one such advertisement appeared in a daily paper in London, and many a man who joined the navy during the Great War was presented with a caul as his mascot.

Another belief is that so long as the caul is in existence it shows the exact state of health of the person who was born with it, no matter how distant that person may be. If he is alive and well the caul is firm and crisp, but it becomes soft and limp if the owner is sick or dead.

Levinus Lemnius in his " Occult Miracles of Nature " says that if the caul at birth be blackish in colour it is a sign of ill fortune for the child, but if it is red the omen is remarkably good.

CERES

The Roman name for the Greek goddess, Demeter, who presided over the fruits of the earth. Anything in her likeness is a mascot for farmers or gardeners, and would form an ideal gift to a friend starting a new venture connected with agriculture.

CHERRY

Cherry-shaped charms or ornaments are fortunate as gifts between friends or lovers. Because the cherry is the tree of Venus these charms procure the protection of the goddess.

To gather cherry blossom is unlucky, but the cherry tree is a mascot. If planted near a house it will bring good fortune to all within the walls, and lovers will never be more fortunate than if they happen to meet for the first time under a cherry tree.

CHILDREN (Special Mascots for)

All mascots which watch over children or attract good health and fortune to them, are in some way connected with Isis, the Universal Mother.   See Amber, Beads, Beans, Bells, Bes, Billiken, Cat's Eye, Caul, Colour, Coral, Crescent, Cybele, Days, Eggs, Elder, Emerald, Hand, Hotei, Key, Knife, Salt, Stork, and Teeth. ,

CHRYSELUTUM

The name of the golden yellow kind of amber (which see). Chryselutum is particularly powerful to ward off or to cure ague.

CHRYSOBERYL

See Cat's Eye.

CHRYSOLITE

The birth stone of Leo, though fortunate to Sagittarius folk also, but must be strictly avoided by those under Pisces.

It is a beautiful stone, often mistaken for a topaz, and is called by different names according to its colour. When yellowish green it is the chrysolite, the name coming from two Greek words " yellow stone," while when of so deep a green as to resemble an emerald it is the Peridot, an Arab name meaning " The Precious One." When its tint is olive green it becomes the Olivine.

In all these forms it was esteemed by the ancients as a protection against evil spirits, while when set in gold was worn as a charm against nightmare.   The mere possession of the stone bestowed occult powers, hence it was sought for by astrologers and seers.   Also it gave eloquence and cured stuttering or other impediments in the speech.

CHRYSOPRASE

The birth stone of Gemini, but unfortunate to people born under Aries or Virgo. It bestows the gifts of sweet temper and hopefulness.

Beads or other ornaments made of chrysoprase may be bought in almost any colour as it takes dyes readily, but in its natural state it is either green or greenish white.

CLAW

The claw of a tiger is a mascot giving its wearer strength and cunning, and it is specially fortunate to those who indulge in gambling or play any games of chance. The claw of an eagle or other large bird uplifts the thoughts and gives ambition and power if carried as a mascot.

CLAY

In many parts of Africa, particularly in the Congo, certain kinds of clay are used with which to daub the fetishes, without the clay the figures being thought powerless.

CLOVER

The finder of a four leaved clover will be fortunate, though in no sense has the plant the wide powers of the shamrock, which see. Yet it is of the four-leafed clover an old country rhyme says :—

> One leaf for fame,
> And one leaf for wealth,
> And one for a faithful lover,
> And one to bring you glorious health
> Are all in a four leaf clover.

COAL

A piece of coal is a very powerful mascot if picked up in the street or given by a friend. It is particularly fortunate as a gift carried over a threshold on New Year's Day. In Yorkshire it is common to see little heaps of coal placed on the doorsteps on New Year's Eve ready for New Year's Day. When that comes each person entering the house picks up one of those lumps of coal and brings it indoors, confident that by doing so good fortune is being assured to those within the house.

COCK

The symbol of watchfulness, and therefore of protection, in which form it is placed on the weather vanes of our churches.

The cock is introduced into many mythologies. It was the companion of Odin and of Jupiter, and figures made to represent it were worn to promote watchfulness and foresight, as in the case of the Abraxas stone.

COCK CROWING

In the West country if a cock comes to the door of a house and gives a sudden crow it is taken as the warning that a stranger approaches, while in many parts of England the persistent crowing of cocks between dusk and midnight is said to foretell a death.

That belief contradicts the Persian which says cocks should crow at nine and twelve in the morning and at night. If they do this their owners may expect sudden good fortune.

COCK'S EYE

In India a favourite mascot is in the shape of the eye of a cock, or often the actual eye of a dead bird is carried. The mascot is worn hung round the neck to ensure watchfulness against threatened danger.

COINS

LUCKY COIN

Very ancient coins bear sacred inscriptions or mystic symbols, therefore they are mascots or luck bringers in the truest sense of the word. Thus the idea of " lucky coins " grew, though in our modern money no coin retains its mystic character excepting the florin with its cross. It is commonly said that if a florin is kept in a purse the devil—*i.e.*, the devil of poverty—will not enter, a tribute to the power of the cross, though the words may be read in a more material sense as well.

The lucky coin with which gamblers toss is a relic of those others coins with their symbolic designs. See pennies.

The illustration is of a coin of King John (A.D. 1199—1216), and should be a typically "lucky coin," since it bears the upright triangle and a crude form of the Star and Crescent.

COLOURS

In the following list of colours with their astrological influences " black " and " white " have been included for the sake of convenience.

BLACK

This being the " colour " of Saturn it is fortunate for those who come within the influence of that mystic planet, especially if they are born under Capricorn, Aquarius, or Libra. These people work their best and play their best when wearing dark shades, and their choice of rooms should be those with dark walls.

Black is unlucky for children's wear, as Saturn is antagonistic to all young creatures, hence the saying that if a young child is dressed in black without special cause, it will lose some near relative and "have to go into mourning " as the phrase is. This is a modern variation of the old belief, for black was unknown as mourning wear until about four centuries ago, but it is easy to understand how it has grown from that far older teaching that black must be kept from children, that everything must be done to save young things from Saturn's influence.

BLUE

Blue is the colour of Venus—and, in its paler shades, of Mercury—but because it is the colour of the summer sky it has been connected with all that is celestial and beautiful. To the Druids it was the sacred colour and it is sacred still, since it is the colour of the Holy Virgin—in direct succession to Venus, Diana, and Isis.

On the other hand, Venus, as goddess of love, had a particularly earthly aspect when under the influence of

Taurus, and thus we trace the slang use of the word
"blue" which has a meaning easy to understand in such
a connection.

We may leave that side of the question, however, to
deal with the traditions which show blue as the colour of
happy lovers. Astrology says all who come under the
influence of Venus by birth date, should wear blue constantly, any shade being fortunate. Mercury's people will
find the colour harmonious also, though for them the
paler tints are best.

We find blue taking part in almost endless legends regarding courtship and marriage. For instance, in
Leicestershire and Lancashire they tell you that on her
wedding day a bride should wear :—

> Something old,
> Something new,
> Something borrowed,
> Something blue.

Yet in the North Riding a bride is warned against
being dressed entirely in blue, since there they have the
rhyme which runs :—

> If dressed in blue
> She's sure to rue.

Probably this was an early Christian teaching, a protest
against the older faiths.

In the south of England you will be told :—

> Those dressed in blue
> Have lovers true.

Whilst all over the country the children chant :—

> Green is forsaken,
> Yellow's forlorn,
> Blue is the luckiest
> Colour that's worn.

A writer in " The Antiquary " (January, 1880) tells us :
" It is remarkable the mention of it (the colour blue)
in connection with folk medicine is so scanty. In 1635 a
man in the Orkney Isles was, we are led to believe, ruined

by nine knots cast on a blue thread and given to his sister. We can understand this, for if a colour possessed mysterious properties, it was quite as certain that they would be diverted if possible into channels of hurt as of healing. On the banks of the Ale and the Teviot to the present day, however, the women have a custom of wearing round their necks blue woollen threads or cords till they wean their children, doing this for the purpose of averting ephemeral fevers. These (sic) are handed down from mother to daughter, and esteemed in proportion to their antiquity. Probably these threads had originally received some blessing or charm and this we should suppose to have been the properly coloured thread to receive such a blessing—for was not blue the Virgin's own colour? We have therefore here two illustrations of the current of people's thoughts. In the Orkneys the blue thread was used for an evil purpose because such a colour savoured of Popery and priests; in the northern counties it was used as a sovereign charm because the remembrance of its once pre-eminent nature still survived in the minds of those who wore it unconsciously, though still actively influencing their thoughts. . . . In German folk-lore lightning is represented as blue."

The fact that blue was the colour sacred to Isis makes plain the wearing of the blue threads by these nursing mothers.

Brown

This is one of the dark shades which are fortunate to those born under Cancer, Libra, Scorpio and Capricorn. As a rule russet brown is the most fortunate shade, except to those who come under Cancer, who should choose the very lightest tint, such as that usually called " fawn."

Green

The wide-spread belief that green is unlucky to all except those born under Cancer, Leo or Sagittarius seems to have originated from the idea that green is the colour of the " little people "—that is, the fairies—who take offence if anyone not entitled to the colour dared to wear it. And the offence was doubly great if the green were mixed with white.

In the " Lady of the Lake " Scott writes :—
— who may dare on wold to wear
The fairies' fatal green?

In his notes to the same poem he writes :—

" As the Daoine Shi or Men of Peace—*i.e.*, fairies—
wore green habits they were supposed to take offence
when any mortals ventured to assume their favourite
colour. Indeed for some reason which has been perhaps
a general superstition, green is held in Scotland to be
unlucky to particular tribes and counties. The Caithness
men who hold this belief allege as a reason that their
bands wore this colour when they were cut off at the
battle of Flodden; and for the same reason they avoid
crossing the Ord on a Monday, being the day of the
week on which their ill-omened array set forth. Green
is also disliked by those of the name of Ogilvy; but more
especially is it held fatal to the whole clan of Graham.
It is remembered of an ancient gentleman of that name
that when his horse fell in a fox chase he accounted for
it by observing that the whipcord attached to his lash
was of this unlucky colour."

Yet, as we all know, green is the colour for Ireland and
all Irishmen. A seeming contradiction which maintains
the whole doctrine of good or evil luck—what is beneficial
to one person is harmful to another.

In most parts of England the prejudice against green
takes the form of saying that if a person wears green
to-day he or she will put on black to-morrow—meaning
that some one near and dear will die.

Another belief is that those to whom green is unfortunate, invariably have an instinctive warning in their
inborn dislike of the colour. But this ill luck seems to
belong to manufactured articles only. In the green of
leaf or bud there is no ill fortune, nor does it appear to
be unlucky to wear artificial leaves however green they
may be. Perhaps the fairies forgive that or even take
it as a compliment.

In " Love's Labour Lost " (Act I. Scene 2) Shakespeare
makes Armado say :—" Green is indeed the colour of

lovers," but the statement is so at variance with every tradition that we may take it the word " green " was either a slip of the pen or a misprint for " blue," unless indeed it is an allusion to the fact that green stands for jealousy, and thus the line means that jealousy and love are intermingled.

Here are a few old folk-rhymes which show green has been always held to be the colour which brings ill luck in love.

> If you love me, love me true,
> Send me a ribbon, a ribbon of blue.
> If you hate me, let it be seen,
> Send me a ribbon, a ribbon of green.

Yorkshire people say that for a bride to be married in green will bring her bad luck, putting the belief into the couplet :—

> Married in May, kirked in green,
> Bride and Bridegroom won't long be seen.

In Sussex the children sing :—

> Those dressed in blue
> Have lovers true.
> In green and white
> Forsaken quite.

The old rhyme beginning " Green's forsaken " has been quoted already under the heading " Blue."

> " Yellow, yellow, turned up with green
> Is the ugliest colour that ever was seen,"

is a Cornish rhyme.

GREY

Correctly speaking this is not a colour, but it must be mentioned from the tradition that silvery grey is fortunate to those born under Gemini. Also to Pisces folks though it is not their chief " colour."

PURPLE (WITH MAUVE OR VIOLET)

We speak of " the royal purple " for it is the colour of our monarch's robes of state—in every court function and high festival it is used as the symbol of kingly power, while in the Church it is the colour of Advent—emblem of the coming of the King.

This is a reminder of the era when purple was sacred to the great Osiris, and after him was given to Jupiter. Though exceptionally powerful to bring good fortune to those who own it as their colour by right of birth-date, it is unfortunate to Libra people.

RED

Red is the fortunate colour to those who come under the influence of the planets Mars or Jupiter. Other people, particularly those born under Libra or Taurus, find that bright red has an irritating effect and rouses their anger. By which it would seem probable that the saying " a red rag to a bull " has a deeper significance than the mere annoyance of the animal.

In the Middle Ages a talisman or sigil had double power if it were written in red, and probably the belief that when a soul was sold the bargain had to be signed in blood to make it binding, had its origin in the same idea.

In the East red has been the colour of magic always.

When the Chinese wore pigtails they wove red threads into the plaits to keep away evil influences, and fabrics with red stripes interwoven are favourite garments for Chinese children because red has power to prevent illness.

For the same reasons red is used as the lining of the pockets in many Chinese garments, while all Imperial decrees in China are written in red ink. Incidentally we may remember that our own Royal Seal is affixed in red wax.

Amongst the Maoris red paint and red colouring generally play an important part in the ceremonies attending the death and burial of any great chief. The house in which the dead man had lived is painted with a sort of red ochre, before its door a carved post, also red, is erected. If the corpse rests at any spot on its way to the grave, there a stone or tree is painted red, and the body is wrapped in a red dyed cloth.

In Southern India the crops are protected from blight by the erection of standing stones painted red in each field.

Red is the sacred colour of many African tribes.

In medicine it has played an important part since the earliest times.

The wise women and leeches of long ago saw in red the representation of heat. Thus they said scarlet clothing was warmer than any other and that scarlet flannel would cure rheumatism when other flannel had failed. Pettigrew in his " Superstitions Connected With the History and Practice of Medicine and Surgery " tells us :—

" We find that in smallpox red bed coverings were employed with a view of bringing the pustules to the surface of the body."

He goes on to tell us that when the son of Edward II. was sick of the smallpox, John of Gaddesdon directed all the bed furniture should be red—a treatment which was so successful the prince recovered without any disfigurement. The Emperor Francis I., father of Marie Antoinette, was wrapped in scarlet blankets when found to be suffering from smallpox, but in his case the treatment was unavailing, for he died.

A Japanese authority, also quoted by Pettigrew, said that when the children of the Royal House were attacked by smallpox they were laid in a chamber that had red walls, were covered with red blankets, and a rule was made that all who approached them must be clothed in red from head to foot.

Mr William George Black, writing in "The Antiquary," tells us that :—

" Red cords and red bands play an important part in modern folk-lore. In the West Indies a little bit of scarlet cloth, however narrow a strip, will keep off whooping cough, and many centuries ago in England we read that for a lunatic one should take of the clove wort ' and wreath it with a red thread about the man's neck when the moon is on the wane in the month that is called April; soon he will be healed.' In the present day to prevent nose bleeding people are told to wear a skein of scarlet silk round the neck tied with nine knots down the front.

If the patient be a man the silk is to be put on and the knots tied by a woman, and if the patient is a woman these good services being rendered her by a man.

"In the West of Scotland it is common—or was so— to wrap a piece of red flannel round the neck of a child in order to ward off whooping cough. The virtue, our informant is careful to tell us, 'lay not in the flannel but in the red colour.'

"Red was the colour symbolical of triumph and victory over all enemies.

"We have evidence of the even recent use of scarlet with a sympathetic purpose in the testimony of a correspondent of "Notes and Queries," who writes :—' When I was a pupil at St. Batholomew's forty years ago, one of our lecturers used to say that within a recent period there were exposed for sale in a shop in Fleet Street red tongues—*i.e.*, tongues of red cloth—to tie round the throats of patients smitten with scarlet fever.' "

WHITE

Stands as the emblem of purity, and it was with that idea that the ancients dedicated it to Virgo—the Virgin. As a colour—if such it may be called—it belongs to those born under that sign, but many silvery shades that may practically be described as white, are fortunate to Gemini people, and also to those of Pisces. Also white belongs to the moon in particular and thus is exceptionally fortunate to "moon folk," another instance of the early worship of Isis, and how her influence has come down to us through so many other faiths.

Rather curiously, white animals are considered unlucky.

In many parts of the country a white cat is called the sign of ill fortune, while in the Midlands they say you must be sure to spit if you meet a white horse face to face, spitting being a powerful spell to avert evil. See Horse.

And in Northamptonshire the unexpected sight of a white mouse is the sure forerunner of a death in the family.

YELLOW

The colour of gold, the colour of the sun, belongs to Ra, the sun god, a form of the great Osiris. All who came under the influence of the sun or who were born under the sign of Leo or Sagittarius will find yellow fortunate, while Cancer folk will benefit if they use it as a secondary colour.

To those born under Taurus or Virgo, yellow will be absolutely unfortunate. Evidently it is of them the old rhyme is speaking when it makes the statement that " yellow's forlorn."

CONCH SHELL

See Shell.

CONFETTI

In Saxon times, and indeed till long afterwards, the path of a bride was strewn with red and white rose leaves —to represent the passion and purity of love. Wheat was another bridal offering, but later rice was used at weddings, a Chinese custom, probably adopted because rice was easy to obtain. Recently the idea was spread that the use of rice was wasteful and even dangerous, thus confetti was invented to take the place of the older rose leaves, and confetti when flung in the air and falling in coloured clouds gives a very pretty effect. Also it is the bearer of good wishes and loving thoughts and as such is a very true mascot.

COPPER

The fortunate metal for those born under Taurus or Libra.

Probably this was the first metal put to practical use by primeval man, for prehistoric weapons and utensils of pure copper have been found, while at a later period it was the chief component of bronze. Its name is a corruption of Cyprus. On that island large copper mines were worked and from them the Greeks and Romans obtained their chief supplies.

CORAL

The birth-stone of Taurus and Scorpio, but the special mascot of children and of mothers, and a protection against the evil eye.

In Roman times the coral was dedicated to Venus, but we trace its influence back through far earlier centuries and know that before the first stone of the Eternal City was laid the coral was sacred to Isis. Powdered coral was scattered on tilled fields in Egypt to shield the crops from storm or blight or locusts. Women wore coral as a charm against sterility, and everywhere it was powerful against all spirits of evil.

Medicinally coral had power also. Ground to a fine powder and mixed with water it was drunk as a remedy for all internal pains, while when burnt and powdered and mixed with grease to form an ointment, it was infallible in the cure of all ulcers and sores.

Above everything else it was the mascot of childbearing women and of children. A string of coral about a baby's neck kept away all evil influences as well as proving an important cure—or prevention—of fits, whooping cough, and teething troubles.

In Italy it is common to find beads of carved coral worn as talismans against the evil eye, and the fact that coral is so much used in rosary beads is from the lingering tradition of its power against all that is bad. See Evil Eye.

CORNELIAN

The birth-stone of Virgo, a charm to protect from all evil, and to avert fever and ague and kindred disease.

The best specimens of cornelian come from India, though all round our coasts fragments of these semi-clear red and yellow and brown stones are to be found. From the days of the ancients the cornelian has been popular for use in signet rings and seals. Its hardness and the high polish it is capable of receiving make it specially suitable for the purpose.

BUCKLE OF ISIS*

Also it was prized because of its occult significance.

* Reprinted by kind permission of William Rider & Son, Ltd., from the "Book of Talismans," by W. T. and K. Pavitt.

In the oldest as well as the more recent Egyptian tombs cornelians have been found, the favourite talisman being in the form of the " Buckle of Isis," a sort of trefoil design bearing a rough resemblance to the shamrock. And almost invariably this buckle—in which we see another reference to the Trinity—was made of cornelian.

During life the Egyptians wore these buckles as talismans to secure the protection of Isis, while after death the buckle was laid on the breast of the corpse that it might ensure a safe journey through the underworld. So important were these cornelian buckles considered that in the Egyptian " Book of the Dead "—which may be called the Testament of the Ancients—there is a whole chapter devoted to the subject.

Amongst Mohammedans this stone is accounted the best for the inscription of sigils and other mystic writings, while deep red specimens are specially chosen to bear quotations from the Koran. In " The Book of Talismans," by W. T. and K. Pavitt, is the statement that :— " In certain districts of Europe under Turkish rule, it was common for the Moslems to take their cornelians to a Christian priest whose blessing was considered to add greatly to their efficiency."

A case of making assurance doubly sure.

White cornelians were popular amongst the ladies of ancient Greece as hair ornaments, and were charms against rheumatism and neuralgia.

In the Middle Ages cornelians were worn as talismans against impure thoughts or evil enchantment, and to act as charms against lightning or fever. Medicinally the stone was considered to have power of staunching the flow of blood.

In China it is held in high esteem as a charm against indigestion and all stomach troubles still.

CORNUCOPEA

Silver charms in the shape of the Cornucopea or Horn or Plenty—a horn filled to overflowing with fruit and flowers—are fairly common, and are intended to be worn on watch chain or bangle to promote success in business and general prosperity. Also they are particularly fortunate for expectant mothers who should wear them to ensure safe delivery and bonnie children.

Tradition says the Cornucopea commemorates the gift Jupiter gave his nurse in gratitude for the milk of a goat with which she fed him. It was a goat's horn he gave her, but endowed with magic powers so that she could obtain from it whatever she wished.

Also it was the symbol of Fortuna, goddess of Fortune, from whom were derived riches and poverty, pleasure and pain, joy or unhappiness, according to her caprice. In ancient monuments she is shown with one, or sometimes two, of these horns of plenty in her hands. Generally she is blindfolded and has a wheel, the sign of Inconstancy.

CORNUCOPEA

COW

See Isis.

CRAB

As a mascot the crab gives courage and perseverance, and helps in conquering difficulties, for in Greek mythology when Hercules had offended Juno he was punished by being injured by a crab, in gratitude for which good service the crab was placed amongst the constellations by the goddess.

Most antiquaries believe that the crab is another form of the beetle or scarab (which see), but on the other hand, it has been called the emblem of the sun, and the fact that a certain portion of the heavens has been given its name is taken as proof of ancient astronomical knowledge. When the sun enters the House of Cancer the Crab, it has reached the limit of its northern declination. Therefore it appears to remain stationary for a few days and them to move in a backward direction. The fact that a crab moves sideways if not exactly backwards, is believed to have led the creature being chosen to represent the sun at that particular period of the year. See Zodiac.

CRANE

In Japan a sacred bird, and as a mascot the giver of health and long life.

CRESCENT

STAR AND CRESCENT

The symbol of Isis, the special mascot of mothers and children and of all young things.

To realize the meaning of this mascot we must go back to the earliest known faith of Ancient Egypt, when men saw in the crescent—the new moon—the symbol of Isis, the mother goddess. Everywhere her faith spread, and many countries adopted her sign, often with a star between the two points of the circle. In Arabia and Central Asia the symbol was known long, long after the worship of Isis had ceased. When the Turks took Constantinople they found the same symbol at the base of the statue of Isis —under the name of Hecate—who was the ancient guardian of the city. The conquering hordes saw an omen of good in the fact that a symbol so familiar to them should be in the city, and they adopted it as their special sign, as it remains to-day.

The illustration is from an Algerian mascot, curiously worked in gold wire.

In Rome young married women wore silver crescents on their shoes to ensure having healthy children.

CRICKET OR GRASSHOPPER

Both these little creatures are symbols of good fortune, particularly in money matters. Charms in their likeness bring success in business, while to hear the creatures chirping in the grass or beside the house, is a promise of good luck. On no account must they be hurt or driven away. To kill a cricket or grasshopper will entail dire misfortune.

CROSS

As an emblem of occult and sacred mysteries the Cross was venerated long before the Christian era, and crosses have been found amongst the remains of the oldest races of man of whom we have knowledge.

The influence of the Cross is world-wide. When the Spaniards landed in Mexico they were amazed to discover that the Indians, who had never heard of Christianity, held the cross as their most sacred symbol. To them it was the sign of the god of Rain, a very merciful deity in the salt wastes of Central America.

No better words to describe the cross can be used than those of Justin the Martyr, who wrote in the second century when the attitude of prayer was to stand with the arms outstretched. He says :—

"The sign of the cross is impressed on the whole of nature. There is hardly a handicraftsman also but uses the figure of it amongst the implements of his industry. It forms part of man himself as may be seen when he raises his hands in prayer."

PREHISTORIC CROSSES

Crosses with direct religious significance are of all shapes. The swastika, perhaps the oldest talisman in the world, is a form of cross with its arms turned back, and swastikas are found in prehistoric remains all over the world. In some of the Egyptian tombs crosses have been discovered that can only be likened to corkscrews with elaborate ring handles—the ring being the sign of Eternity crowning the cross.

THE CROSS OF SACRIFICE

Death on the cross was the method by which sacrifices were offered to Baal, not only human beings suffering thus, but animals as well, though the general idea was that only the best and most valued of its kind should be offered. The Carthaginians were worshippers of Baal, and when their general, Malcus, wished to secure the favour of the god, he clothed his best beloved son in royal robes and crucified him as a sacrifice!

The Phœnicians—Baal worshippers also—used the cross in the same way. Thus it became the symbol of Sacrifice in which connection crosses have been found amongst the remains of long dead civilizations in places so far apart as Assyria, Egypt, Persia, India, and Scandinavia.

THE LATIN CROSS

The cross with which we are most familiar is the Latin and of that, especially with regard to its sacred significance, nothing need be said here.

THE GREEK CROSS

The Greek Cross, with its four arms of equal length, was adopted as the sign of the Greek Church in distinction from that of Rome, but the Greek Cross is to be found on many of our ceremonial orders, notably surmounting the orb used at the Coronation of the King.

THE MALTESE CROSS

Was a heraldic design, the badge of the Kinghts of Malta, and other orders.

SAINT GEORGE'S CROSS

Practically a Greek Cross, emblazoned in crimson on a blue ground, as a badge of English knighthood, and worn in honour of St. George the patron saint.

SAINT ANDREW'S CROSS

Can only be described as resembling the letter X. It is the sign of Scotland, and was adopted in honour of Saint Andrew whose relics rest in that country. The saint suffered martyrdom on a cross of this shape.

THE CROSS OF SAINT BENEDICT

This was a very popular mascot, guarding its wearer against all sorts of danger. It was engraved on a metal disc, with certain letters, each standing for a Latin word so that the whole formed a prayer.

IRISH CROSS

This is a form of the Wheel Cross, which see.

THE CROSS AS A SIGNATURE

In the popular "Faith, Hope and Charity" sets of charms the cross stands as an emblem of Faith. So it is, but it was a powerful talisman against every form of evil, hence came the custom of affixing a cross to a document in place of the signature of anyone who could not write— the cross being used prevented the signature being put to any ill purpose.

THE TAU CROSS

Probably the most ancient of all forms of crosses— excepting perhaps the swastika—is the Tau Cross, so called from its likeness to the Greek letter of that name, and indeed it can best be described as resembling our own capital T. It consists of an upright bar with a shorter bar, laid across the top, and was a very early sign of authority carried by priests and chiefs or their representatives, as the sceptre of the king, the crozier of the bishop, or the baton of a field-marshal are borne to-day.

In the Greek Church it is the Tau Cross the Metropolitan or bishop carries still, and we have it lingering in a debased form in the mallet of the auctioneer or the hammer used by the chairman at public meetings. We see these as means of recording bids or as demands for silence, but all the same they are the sign of authority and direct descendants of the Tau Cross of mystic power.

Crosses in this shape were worn as charms against diseases of the skin and inflammatory poisons, but particularly against the bites of snakes. It was on a Tau Cross that Moses raised the brazen serpent in the wilderness, making use of the lessons he had learnt in Egypt, where this particular form of cross was venerated as a healer.

Also the Tau Cross was the sign of Life, and as such it was used by the Romans. After a battle when the roll was called, a Tau Cross was set against the names of those who answered. It became the symbol of life and safety, and as such was worn as a charm.

The Jews used it as part of various magic ceremonies which they used to cure erysipelas, and when St. Anthony the Copt devoted himself to the care of sufferers from that disease (since called St. Anthony's Fire in his honour) he adopted the Tau Cross as his sign. In the eleventh century erysipelas had become such a scourge in Europe that an Order of Friars made it the work of their lives to fight the disease. They wore black habits with the Tau Cross worked in blue upon their breasts.

In Ancient Egypt it stood as the sign of Thoth, god of Wisdom, and belonged to all who studied mysteries or the art of healing.

Charms for personal wear were made of it and when it formed a handle, as it were, to a dangling heart, it was a protection from evil spirits. When instead of a heart a ring was attached to it, it stood as the emblem of Eternal Safety.

WHEEL CROSS

WHEEL CROSS

Another very ancient cross is the Wheel Cross —a circle within which is one or more crosses of four arms each, forming a star. This was used on the shields of soldiers and appeared in ancient temples as the symbol of the Sun. The Druids— who amongst much other learning knew the true position of the heavenly bodies—used it in the same way. To them the centre was the sun, the radiating lines the planets, and the surrounding circle stood for Infinity or Eternity.

Charms in this shape are common in Northern Europe where such a device is often built into the walls of a house as an ornament in these days though originally it was a protection against fire. With us the Wheel Cross lingers chiefly as the round brass ornament that appears on the harness of carthorses and hangs between the eyes. Originally its purpose was to defend the animal and his rider from the power of the Evil Eye. The illustration

shows a form of the Wheel Cross on a coin of Edward
the Elder (A.D. 901—925).

CRUTCHES

Talismans which resemble a tau cross in shape but are
called crutches are popular in the East. Invariably they
form an elongated letter or group of letters which make
a word—usually the name of some prophet or saint. See
Sigil.

CRYSTAL

Have the same powers as the Cat's Eye, which see.
They influence the same birth dates. Beads of crystal
are worn as the cure for dropsy in the East.

CUCKOO

" I'll have no luck this year, I've never so much as
heard the cuckoo once all through the spring," an old
woman said to the writer, and the idea that when you first
hear the cuckoo you must " wish and turn your money "
is widespread. Brand is rather tantalizing concerning
this bird, for he quotes one Werenfels who he calls " an
old writer " as saying :—

" If the superstitious man has any desire to know how
long he will live he consults the cuckoo."

There the statement stops. We are not told how the
information may be obtained.

CUPID

The lover's mascot, the bringer of good fortune to
sweethearts.

This is the Latin name of the Greek Eros, of whom
Cupid is a less lofty form. Eros is the god of Love
indeed, but it was love in its highest sense, while Cupid
is rather an earthbound little fellow, as might be expected
from his being the son and the constant companion of
Venus. In Roman art he was generally shown as a mis-
chievous boy with bow and arrows and wings. Sometimes he carries a burning torch with which he lights the
fire of love, but as a rule he contents himself with his
arrows, using the latter to transfix two hearts and thus
bind them together.

CUSHION

See Pillow.

CYBELE

A Greek deity who was variously described as "the ancient mother," "the great mother," and "mother of the gods," and thus may be identified with one of the forms of Isis. In art she is represented seated on a throne with lions crouching on either hand, or else she is in a chariot drawn by lions. She is a very earthbound goddess, but a mascot to mothers and young children.

CYCLAMEN

Pliny says this pretty flower ought to be planted near every home because where it grows no poisons can have power.

DAIKOKU

The Japanese god of love, the guardian angel of sweethearts, the inspirer of tender thoughts. He is the god of wealth also, and is represented as carrying a hammer, a symbol of power.

DAISY

The daisy is one of the plants which astrologers call " under Venus." Probably that is why the marguerite is chosen for the love charm by which a girl counts the petals, saying in turn :—" He loves me—he loves me not."

The flowers are mascots to those who are pure in thought and loyal in love, and a bunch of daisies given by one friend to another induces a happy frame of mind. A daisy root has power to bring back an absent lover if a girl sleeps with it under her pillow—so the Hampshire gipsies say.

DART

See Arrow.

DAYS

In " Grafton's Manual," published in 1565, is the following list of unlucky days, but it is not stated clearly whether they were unlucky during that year alone or were to be tabooed for all time :—

"January 1, 2, 4, 5, 10, 15, 17, 29.
February 26, 27, 28.
March 16, 17, 20.
April 7, 8, 10, 20.
May 3, 6, 7, 15, 20.
June 4, 8, 10, 22.
July 15, 21.
August 1, 19, 20, 29, 30.
September 2, 4, 6, 7, 21, 23.
October 4, 6, 16, 24.
November 5, 6, 15, 20, 29, 30.
December 6, 7, 9, 15, 22.

Quaint advice as to three days in the year on which no new business must be started was given by Lord Burghley in a letter to his son, dated 1633, gravely bringing forward the reasons why these were days when nothing new should be begun. They were :—

The first Monday in April, because it was then that Cain was born, and also the day on which he killed his brother!

The second Monday in August, being the day on which the Cities of the Plain were destroyed!!

The last Monday in December, because it was the birthday of Judas Iscariot!!!

Where his Lordship obtained his information is not stated, but it is probable the days so marked were connected with some tradition of long pre-Christian times to which these Biblical events had been attached later.

In "The Book of Knowledge," published early in the eighteenth century and quoted by Brand, appears the following :—

"Account of the Perillous Dayes of Every Month— In the change of every moon be two days in the which what thing soever is begun, late or never it shall come to no good end. And the dayes be full perillous for many things."

The book goes on to give these unlucky days as follows :—

" In January when the moon is three or four days old.
February when the moon is five or seven days old.
March when the moon is six or seven days old.
April when the moon is five or eight days old.
May when the moon is eight or nine days old.
June when the moon is five or fifteen days old.
July when the moon is three or thirteen days old.
August when the moon is eight or thirteen days old
September when the moon is eight or thirteen days old.
October when the moon is five or twelve days old.
November when the moon is five or nine days old.
December when the moon is three or thirteen days old."

Of the special beliefs and traditions concerning the seven days of the week, the following is an account. The connection between each day and an astrological influence is easy to trace when the meaning of the name by which we know the day is considered.

SUNDAY

The day sacred to the Sun stands for all that is full of light and power and which gives life. Also the sun was—and is—the symbol of Eternity, of the rising again after death.   With Teutonic nations the sun is called feminine; it is the mother, the Isis, who brings forth light, but with the Egyptians it is Osiris, the father, and thus we, following Egyptian teaching, speak of the sun as " he."

Children born on a Sunday have many good gifts. Love of colour and brightness will be theirs, and they have the inborn joy of what we term sunny natures. They should wear charms made of gold.

MONDAY

The Moon's day, and the influence of the moon on those born at her special festival gives beauty and imagination. For a child born on a Monday all silver charms are fortunate, and the crescent—the sign of Isis—should be worn.   In the mythology of Northern Europe the moon was a male deity, a brave warrior who was given to fits of brooding melancholy.

TUESDAY

Named after Twi, the Norse Mars, the god of war. Those born on a Tuesday will find cornelian their lucky stone.

WEDNESDAY

The day of Odin or Woden, the Norse Jupiter, though most authorities say that Odin was a form of Mercury, apparently for no other reason than that Mercury's day was given as that which came in the middle of the week by the Romans, hence the French call it by his name still. But Odin was the king of the gods; he wore the eagle's wings on his helmet and the eagle was Jupiter's bird. Surely, then, it is Jupiter who rules over Wednesday, though we find his influence acknowledged in the following day as well.

THURSDAY

Thor's Day, and Thor was the great Norse god who wielded the mighty hammer that has been identified with the thunderbolt of Jupiter.

Thor was the god of unrest. Many travellers have been born on this day—hence the line in the old rhyme, " Thursday's bairn has far to go." The Swastika charm, Thor's hammer, should be worn by all travellers.

FRIDAY

This is often called an unlucky day, yet according to astrology it is quite the reverse, especially to lovers. It is named after Freiya, the Norse goddess of love and marriage, therefore the Scottish custom of making it the favourite day for weddings is correct.

SATURDAY

It is generally stated this is " Saturn's day," and as Saturn was the god of workers we may trace that belief in the rhyme with its " Saturday's bairn works hard for a living," but many authorities, including Sharon Turner, point out that the Norsemen knew nothing of Saturn, therefore his name could not have come to us from them, though all our day names are purely Norse.

Mr Turner suggests the name comes from Surtur's Day—a day for finishing up—or settling down.

In Norse mythology the gods fought with monsters named Surtur from Muspelheim, and in the mighty conflict the world came to an end, only to wake again and begin a new era of greater beauty. Geologists may trace in this some vague memory of one or other of the mighty cataclysms that have engulfed the globe at various stages, while the end of the week and the end of a period in the world's story being connected in festival, is easy to understand.

A very old rhyme refers to the best day on which to remove house or to start a new business and runs :—

> Monday for health,
> Tuesday for wealth,
> Wednesday the best day of all.
> Thursday for crosses,
> Friday for losses,
> Saturday no luck at all.

Here is another old rhyme :—

> Sneeze on a Monday,
> You get a letter;
> Sneeze on a Tuesday,
> You get something better;
> Sneeze on a Wednesday,
> You sneeze for danger;
> Sneeze on a Thursday,
> Meet a stranger;
> Sneeze on a Friday,
> Sneeze for sorrow;
> Sneeze on a Saturday,
> See your best friend to-morrow.

Then as to birthdays, we are told :—

> Monday's bairn is fair of face,
> Tuesday's bairn is full of grace;
> Wednesday's bairn is child of woe,
> Thursday's bairn has far to go;
> Friday's bairn is loving and giving,
> Saturday's bairn works hard for a living;

The bairn that is born on a Sabbath day
Is lucky and bonny and wise and gay.

Most people know the old rhyme about washing
clothes :—

If you wash on Monday,
    You've all the week to dry;
If you wash on Tuesday,
    You've let a day go by;
If you wash on Wednesday,
    There's half the week away;
If you wash on Thursday,
    You choose an awkward day;
If you wash on Friday,
    It is because you need;
If you wash on Saturday,
    You are a slut indeed.

Then there is a rhyme as to the cutting of nails :—

Cut your nails on Monday—
Cut them for news;
Cut your nails on Tuesday—
A new pair of shoes;
Cut your nails on Wednesday—
Cut them for health;
Cut your nails on Thursday—
Cut them for wealth;
Cut your nails on Friday—
Cut them for woe;
Cut your nails on Saturday—
A journey to go;
Cut your nails on Sunday—
You'll cut them for evil,
For all through the week
You'll be ruled by the devil.

DEER

The picture or model of a stag or any kind of deer is
an important Chinese talisman to secure success in a
business or profession for which study is required.

Yet for some unknown reason—unless it is from the
fact that deer have horns, and horns were one of the

distinguishing features of Satan according to the early
Christians—in many parts of England it is unlucky to
have a live deer cross your path, particularly if it goes
from right to left.

DIAGRAM

See Sigil.

DIAMOND

The birth-stone of Aries and Scorpio, and of all who
come under the influence of Mars.

The ancients taught that the diamond was the most
powerful of all jewels in its influence against the powers
of evil, and even to-day the sprinkling of diamond dust
on the child is part of the baptismal ceremony amongst
the wealthy Hindus, the idea being that a child so
sprinkled will grow up virtuous.

A very ancient belief says that in order to exercise its
full power a diamond must be worn on the left side of
the body, and so set that it touches the skin—hence the
custom of placing diamond rings on the left hand and
having what is called the clear setting of the gem.

Our old friend, Sir John Maundeville, explains the
reason of this as follows :—

" A man should carry a diamond on his left side, for it
is of greater virtue than on the right side; for the strength
of their growing is towards the north, that is the left side
of the world and the left part of a man when he turns his
face to the east. And if you wish to know the virtues of
the diamond . . . I shall tell you as they beyond the
sea say and affirm, from whom all science and philosophy
comes. He who carries the diamond upon him, it gives
him hardiness and manhood, and it keeps the limbs of his
body whole. It gives him victory over his enemies in
court and in war, if his cause be just; and it keeps him
that bears it in good wit; and it keeps him from strife and
riot, and from sorrows and enchantments, and from fan-
tasies, and the illusions of evil spirits. And if any cursed
witch or enchanter should bewitch him who bears a
diamond, all that sorrow and mischance shall turn to the
offender through the virtue of the stone, and also no wild

beast dare assail a man that bears it on him. Also the diamond should be given freely without coveting and without buying, and then it is of greater value."

There is a persistent tradition that a diamond will have no power for good—indeed it may have exactly the opposite effect—if it is won by fraud or crime. It is only a mascot in the true sense when its owner has pure thoughts and a loyal mind. When the faithless, the degraded, or the criminal possess diamonds the gems are actual bringers of bad luck.

In this connection it is interesting to remember the histories of the greatest diamonds of the world. The Koh-i-Noor was followed by bloodshed and horror through its history till it was presented to Queen Victoria, when the Hindus said its power for evil would go, since so long as it was not owned by a man all would be well. Queen Victoria was supposed to be superior to superstition, but all the same she took care to bequeath the great diamond to the King's Consort in all futurity and not to the King himself.

The Hope Diamond brought ill fortune to all its possessors. It shone on the neck of the Duchess of Montespan, favourite of Louis XIV., and almost as soon as she secured the jewel she lost her royal lover and sank into obscurity. Later it was part of the regalia of Marie Antoinette; after her execution it turned up in the possession of a dealer in Amsterdam, who was robbed by his own son. The father died of starvation and the son committed suicide. The Hope family were purchasers of the diamond, and misfortune dogged their steps till the early part of the present century, when it was sold by Sir Francis Hope. The ex-Sultan, Abdul Hamid, was the' purchaser, and lost his throne; after which the diamond passed into the keeping of a firm of American jewellers, and there has been a rumour that it was bought by a gentleman who was drowned in the Titanic, carrying the jewel with him.

Of the Orloff diamond, part of the late Tsar's regalia, the past history was one of horror, and horrors surround it still.

In the East it is said diamonds should never be worn as buttons by women—to use them for such a purpose is to court violent death. In the published accounts of the murder of the Tsar and his family it is definitely stated the girl princesses had large diamonds hidden in pieces of material and sewn on their dresses as buttons. They were wearing these buttons at the time of the wholesale murder in the cellar.

DISCUS

See Wheel.

DISEASES
(Mascots and Charms to Prevent or Cure)

In nearly every case either a jewel or a sigil is the special mascot to guard against illness, and particulars will be found under separate heads as follows :—

AGUE : See Abracadabra, Bloodstone, Chryselutum and Cornelian.

APOPLEXY : See Lapis Lazuli.

ASTHMA : See Cat's Eye and Topaz.

BITES : See Cross.

CHILDISH COMPLAINTS : See Amber, Coral, Cat's Eye, Silver.

CHOLERA : See Acorn, Coral.

CROUP : See Cat's Eye.

CRAMP : See Rings.

DEAFNESS : See Amber.

DRUNKENNESS : See Amethyst and Sigil.

DROPSY : See Bloodstone, Crystal, Jacinth, and Moonstone.

EYE TROUBLES : See Agate, Elder, Emerald Jade, Lizard, Sapphire.

ERYSIPELAS : See Amber and Tau Cross.

FAINTNESS : See Emerald.

FEVER : See Agate, Cornelian, Garnet, Jacinth, and also under Colours.

FITS : See Coral, Jade, Jet, Lapis Lazuli, Magi Rings, Sigil, Silver, Tau Cross.

GOITRE : See Amber.

GOUT : See Topaz.

HYSTERIA : See Amethyst and Moon.

HEMORRHAGE : See Bloodstone and Cornelian.

HEADACHE : See Turquoise.

INDIGESTION : See Bloodstone, Amber, and Coral.

INFECTION : See Amber, Arrow, Carbuncle, and Lamb.

KIDNEY DISEASE : See Jade, Penny.

LUMBAGO : See Colour.

MEMORY, LOSS OF : See Emerald.

NEURALGIA : See Amethyst and Cornelian.

NERVE TROUBLE : See Amethyst and Cat's Eye.

NIGHTMARE : See Chrysolite and Stone.

NOSE BLEEDING : See Colour (Red) and Knots.

PAIN : See Sardonyx.

POISON : See Amber, Tau Cross, and Cyclamen.

RHEUMATISM : See Cornelian and Malachite.

SEA SICKNESS : See Beryl.

SMALLPOX : See Colour (Red).

SNAKE BITE : See Agate, Tau Cross, Emerald, and Onyx.

SORES AND ULCERS : See Coral and Finger.

STOMACHIC TROUBLES : See Amber, Aquamarine, Beryl, Carbuncle, Coral, Cornelian, Jacinth, and Jade.

TEETH, LOSS OF : See Amber; also under Teeth.

TEETHING : See Amber and Coral.

THROAT TROUBLES : See Aquamarine, Beryl, Carbuncle, and Cat's Eye.

TOOTHACHE : See Aquamarine; also Teeth.

WARTS : See Moon.

WOUNDS : See Agate, Bloodstone, and Carbuncle.

WHOOPING COUGH : See Colour, Coral.

DIVERS (Special Mascot to Protect)
See Pearls.

DOCKS

This very familiar plant belongs to Jupiter, therefore is fortunate if it grows near a house, giving success and power. Also it is the special mascot of young mothers, and the seeds of dock, placed in a little bag and tied round the left arm, help women in labour.

DOGS

Perhaps in recognition of his faithful devotion to man a dog of any kind is a mascot—unless he is an evil spirit which has taken a dog's shape, as the Mauthe Dog of Peele Castle. Some lingering connection with that remains in the nurse's story that a naughty child " has a black dog on his back."

Yet black dogs are true mascots. If a black dog follows you home be sure some good fortune will follow.

To dream of a black dog or to see the likeness of a dog in the fire are both signs that a friend is near, say the gipsies.

DOG MERCURY

This little wild plant has no right to be included in any list of respectable mascots, for it is absolutely unlucky to most people. Vows spoken near a place where it flourishes will not be kept, and if it is brought into a house ill luck will follow it. Yet there is a legend that if a robber or dishonest man of any kind carries a piece of dog mecury his nefarious plans will flourish, so it is the mascot of the evil-doer.

DOLPHIN

A fish sacred to Apollo, therefore a mascot giving success in music or the arts, but also a bringer of good in many ways.

In all the legends of mythology the dolphin is a kindly creature, helping man, and becoming a willing servant of the gods.

The drawing is from an illustration in " The Celestial Atlas," published for private circulation, A.D. 1786.

DOLPHIN

DOORSTEPS

For steps made in gold or silver for use as charms see under the heading of Ladder. But in parts of Wales it is said that a whitened doorstep will bring good fortune to the house as no evil will cross it—probably to this belief we can trace the beginning of the custom of "hearthstoning" the steps.

In many parts of England, particularly in the Midlands, the doorsteps are not whitened but either coloured red all over or decorated by having red patterns drawn on them in wavy lines—a clear survival of the drawing of mystic signs or the writing of sigils.

A broomstick laid across a threshold is a charm against any form of evil—so Hampshire gipsies say.

DOVE

Probably because of its religious significance the dove is seldom or never used as a charm or ornament, yet it is the symbol of peace, and anything made in its likeness should heal quarrels and unite parted friends.

The live bird is fortunate, say the gipsies, who are never more pleased than if a white dove or pigeon alights on the path before them. They will tell you a white dove is a sign of a wedding if it comes frequently to perch on the roof of a house.

On the other hand, there are people who are terrified if a white bird haunts the house, seeing a sign of trouble, while a white bird pecking at a window pane foretells a death, or at least a serious illness within that room. There is more than one family in England whose members are invariably warned of the loss of a relative through the appearance of a white, ghostly bird, so it may be those legends have spread till any white bird is credited with bearing the same sinister news.

DRAGON

A favourite Chinese talisman worn to secure happiness at home and long life. In Thibet dragons are painted on flags which fly over the housetops to bring success in business and good fortune generally.

EAGLE

The symbol that gives courage and success, dignity and power, thus helping the owner to rise to the greatest heights.

In our churches the eagle appears as the symbol of St. John the Evangelist, and in almost all other religions the " king of birds " plays a part. In India the eagle Garuda, was the bearer of the god Vishnu, and carried him in his victories over the powers of darkness. In ancient Greece it was told that when Zeus was preparing for his battle with the Titans, the eagle brought him the thunderbolts by which he was to conquer, and was adopted as the emblem of the god in consequence.

From his lofty flight and the belief that he alone of all living creatures can gaze straight at the noonday sun, the eagle has been taken as typifying the ascension of the soul after death.

In Norse mythology the bird represented the storm instead of the powers which conquered the storm, but Odin wore eagle's wings on his helmet.

Because of its close connection with Jupiter the eagle became the symbol of earthly power, and Ptolemy Soter adopted it as the emblem of the Egyptian kingdom. In ancient Rome it was part of the insignia of the Republic, and all know the use made of it in heraldry.

In China and Japan little eagles cast in metal or carved in stone are carried by soldiers to endow them with fearlessness and strength.

Here at home the figures of stone eagles are seen topping the gate posts of large houses. To-day these are mere ornaments, but originally they were the sign that a person of importance dwelt within.

EBISU

The Japanese god of plenty, giver of all household good, provider of the daily food.

EGGS

Because the egg—itself an inanimate object—holds the germ of life, the earliest thinkers saw in it a symbol of Eternity. Later the Early Christians seized upon it as the sign of Resurrection, in which connection it is used as the familiar Easter gift.

Eggs have been connected with hope and birth and the young from prehistoric times, and in many parts of the country are still popular gifts to carry into any house where a new born baby lies, the gift of eggs ensuring good fortune to mother and child.

Brand tells us :—" Hutchinson observes that ' the egg was a sacred emblem and seems a gift well adapted to infancy.' Bryant says, ' An egg containing in it the elements of life was thought no improper emblem of the ark in which were preserved the elements of the future world; hence in the Dionusiaca, and in other mysteries, one part of the nocturnal ceremony consisted of the consecration of an egg. By this, we are informed by Porphry, was signified the world. It seems to have been a favourite symbol, and very ancient, and we find it adopted by all nations.'

In Yorkshire they say that eggs with white shells are the best to give a friend at Easter, though they may be decorated in colours, but that blue is lucky for lovers, that brown will make one merry, but no egg which has a tinge of green in its shell should ever be given.

Also in Yorkshire it is the custom to " roll eggs " at Easter—at least it was until a few years ago. On Easter Monday the children used to carry baskets of gaily-coloured eggs to the top of steep and grassy hills and roll them down the slope. No particular order was observed, nothing seemed to result from the rolling, and no explanation of the custom was forthcoming.

It would seem to be a survival of a very ancient form of divination. The Druids bound a wheel with straw, then, setting it on fire, sent it rolling down a hill, reading prospects for the future in its progress. If it ran well and truly to the foot of the height success in battle and wealth of crops awaited the nation, but defeat and famine might be expected if the wheel turned aside and fell before it had travelled far. The suggestion that eggs were rolled at the feast of Easter for the same purpose, is mere conjecture, but seems possible.

Strings of wild birds' eggs bring ill luck to any house into which they are carried. Thus in Dorset schoolboys are compelled to keep their collections of eggs hanging in outhouses or on outer walls.

ELEPHANT

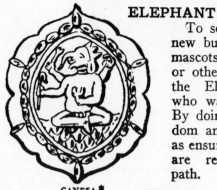

GANESA *

To secure success in **any** new business, Hindus wear mascots shaped as elephants or other effigies of Ganesa, the Elephant-Headed god who was the son of Siva. By doing so they gain wisdom and foresight, as well as ensuring that all obstacles **are** removed from their path.

ELDER

The gipsies call the elder bush the beneficent tree and say all blessings may be obtained from it. Wood, bark, leaves, flowers, and berries, have medicinal value, but chief of its properties is its power over witches and evil spirits who cannot approach a house round which elder bushes grow, nor enter any place where elder is.

A gipsy woman told of a haunted house in which no one could live till a ring of elder bushes was planted round it, then all the hauntings ended, and she finished her story in this fashion :—

" Talkin' of elder trees—only a day or two agone a woman as is believed to have a goodish bit of witch-ways about she, couldn't get through a gate as opens into a garden I knows well. Try how her would, get into it her couldn't, though her had come there most particular with a parcel as the carrier's cart had just brought in. Afterwards her allowed as it was the dogs she was afeared on, but, my dear soul, the elder boughs do hang over that there gate ! "

Yet strangely in many parts of the country the elder is called " the tree of disgrace," and there is a legend that it was upon an elder and not upon what is called the Judas thorn, that Judas hanged himself.

Amongst other beliefs connected with the tree is one

* Reprinted by kind permission of William Rider & Son, Ltd. from the " Book of Talismans," by W. T. and K. Pavitt.

to the effect that a child, or indeed any young creature, will become a dwarf if struck by anger by a bough of elder, its growth being stopped from the moment of the blow.

EMERALD

The gem of the House of Cancer, which is ruled by the moon, the mother-goddess, Isis. Thus the emerald is a particularly fortunate gem for child-bearing women—in olden days the expectant mother was advised to hang an emerald round her neck so that is rested on her breast.

In addition to safeguarding mother and child and preserving the sight, the emerald was worn to prevent its wearer suffering from faintness, or loss of memory. It revealed secrets to its owner (how is not stated), and bestowed the gift of eloquence.

It was the special mascot of sailors and fishermen, protecting them from the perils of the sea, through its association with Isis, the moon, the ruler of tides.

Ancient astrologers named the emerald as the most fortunate gift that could pass between lovers, ensuring constancy and truth, but modern astrologers maintain it should be worn only by those born under Cancer.

Pliny tells us :—" If the sight hath been dimmed and wearied with intense poring over anything, the beholding of an emerald doth refresh and restore it again."

In the East it is regarded as particularly powerful as the preserver of the sight, when a verse from the Koran has been engraved upon it. In Persia it is bound round the left arm with a green string and becomes a special mascot for travellers, preserving them from the powers of a very evil spirit called Deeds.

So powerful are its rays against all evil things that serpents were blinded by the mere sight of the stone. Moore mentions this belief in his " Lalla Rookh," when he describes poor Hinda as having :—

> . . . eyes so pure that from their ray
> Dark vice would turn abashed away,
> Blinded like serpents when they gaze
> Upon the emerald's virgin rays.

It will be noticed that again the influence of the stone is exerted over the eyes. The effect is good for those the Powers that Be consider worthy of help, and bad for everything evil for which the serpent stands.

Modern occultists agree that green is the colour most soothing to the eye. Shades to protect the sight are painted green, the walls of eye hospitals are of the same shade. When a patient's eyes are unbandaged after an operation it is rays of green light which are first allowed to meet his vision.

EROS

See Cupid.

EYE

The exact representation of an eye is practically unknown amongst mascots, but nothing is more common than a design in the shape of a circle set within a larger ring, and this is the direct descendant of the ancient endeavours to give the likeness of an eye.

In Egypt the eye was one of the signs of Ra the Sun god, symbolising his all-seeing power.

A charm roughly made in this pattern was called the Eye of Osiris, and during the process of embalming the dead this was placed inside the body. Its mission was to watch over the soul, and guide it through the darkness to the light beyond.

The eye was found on necklaces worn by the living also, to drive away evil influences and keep its wearer free from witchcraft; indeed it was the special charm against the Evil Eye. Its likeness to the Wheel Cross (which see) and its use for the same purpose cannot be overlooked. Probably the two became confused owing to their resemblance to each other.

Eye of a Cock

Mascot to ensure watchfulness. See **Cock.**

Two Eyes

When two eyes appear side by side in an Egyptian talisman the right eye is the symbol of Osiris and the left of Isis. This talisman was carried to confer physical and mental strength.

EVIL EYE

All over the world the belief in the power of the Evil Eye will be found—that is the certainty that the enemy who wishes ill to another will have those wishes granted by the powers of evil, unless the beneficent spirits can be induced to work against them. In most cases it is thought that the Evil Eye is exerted through jealousy, thus it is considered " unlucky " to praise a child or any young creature openly lest someone—or something—hearing the praise should become envious and wish ill to the child in consequence.

" In the East and also in Southern Europe the use of mascots—or amulets—is to avert misfortune rather than to attract good luck," writes Algernon Warren in " Chambers Journal." " When the writer was in the island of Capri not many years ago, on the terrace of an hotel which is always besieged in the season by smiling women with baskets of coral pins, brooches, etc., he noticed one of these sellers appealing most emphatically to a couple of English visitors who had a pretty child with them, whose golden hair elicited a good deal of outspoken admiration. The English visitors made some purchases from her, but she pressed them to buy a coral necklace for the child. Seeing they were indifferent to her solicitations she took from her basket a coral necklace with a coral charm in the shape of a finger attached to it. This she presented to the child. . . . Subsequently she confided her motive, which showed her belief in the prevalent Eastern superstition that it is unlucky to be praised with particular warmth, and that as the child's beauty was attracting attention someone might cast the evil eye upon her unless she had a coral charm to avert its influence."

Certain mascots were specially used to avert the power of the Evil Eye, to thwart the work of witches, and generally to combat Black Magic. See Abracadabra, Abraxas, Amber, Angel, Arrow, Bacchus, Beans, Bells, Blackthorn, Broomstick, Bulla, Cat, Chrysolite, Crescent, Cross, Doorstep, Eye, Hand, Hanuman, Heart, Horseshoe, Iron, Jet, Jochebed, Lodestone, Ring, Rue, Scales,

Solomon's Seal, Shinenaka, Sigil, Star, Steps, Straw, Teeth, Tiki, Topaz, Tortoise, Wolf.

FAN

In the East the fan is the token of power, and is worn as a charm to bring good health and safety. Little fan-charms are not often seen in our shops, but the writer possesses two of Hindu workmanship. They are of silver, less than an inch in length, but made to open and shut exactly as an ordinary, full-sized fan might do. An English lady, to whom they were given half a century or more ago, had them mounted as ear-rings, but the original intention was that they should be worn round the neck as bringers of good luck.

FARMERS (Special Mascots for)

See Agate, Bloodstone, Ceres, Iron.

FINGER

The reason why the third finger of the left hand—or as it used to be called the fourth finger, reckoning in the thumb—should be chosen as the special ring finger has been the cause of many theories.

In ancient times it was maintained that a nerve or artery—opinions differed as to which it was—passed direct from that finger to the heart, thus the finger was the most closely connected with the seat of life. It was endowed with magical powers, and was generally honoured above all the rest.

As illustration of this theory Levinus Lemnius may be quoted. His book on surgery and medicine was translated into English in 1658.

" . . . a small branch of the arterie, and not of the nerves as Gellius thought, is stretched forth from the heart to this finger, the motion thereof you shall perceive evidently in women with child and wearied in travel and all effects of the heart, by the touch of your fore-finger. I used to raise such as are fallen in a swoon by pinching this joynt and by rubbing the ring of gold with a little saffron, for by this a restoring force that is in it, passeth to the heart and refresheth the fountain of life unto

which this finger is joyn'd : wherefore it deserves honour
above the rest and ambiguity thought fit to encompass it
about with gold. Also the worth of this finger that it
receives from the heart, procured thus much that the old
physicians from whom it hath the name of Medicus,
would mingle their mendicaments and potions with this
finger, for no venom can stick upon the every outmost
part of it but it will offend a man and communicate itself
to his heart."

With the passing of the Middle Ages and the wakening
of what we may call modern knowledge, this idea of the
special properties of the third finger came to be contra-
dicted. Thus in 1708 a correspondent wrote to the
magazine, the " British Apollo," to ask the editor why
wedding rings were worn on that special finger, and was
replied to thus :—

" There is nothing more in this than that the custom
was handed down to the present age from the practice of
our ancestors who found the left hand more convenient
for such ornaments than the right, in that it is ever less
employed; for the same reason they chose the fourth
(third) finger which is not only less used than either or
the rest but is more capable of preserving the ring from
bruises, having this quality peculiar to itself that it
cannot be extended but in company with some other
finger, whereas the rest may stretched to their full length
and straightness. Some of the ancients were of opinion
in this matter that the ring was so worn because to that
finger, and to that only, comes an artery from the heart;
but the politer knowledge of our modern anatomists
having clearly demonstrated the absurdity of the notion,
we are rather inclined to believe the continuance
of the custom is owing to the reason above
mentioned."

In the early Christian Church, according to the missals
of York and Lincoln, at the marriage ceremony the bridegroom had to place the ring first on the bride's thumb,
then upon her first finger, then on her second, and lastly,
on the third, where it was to remain. This seems a
reminder of the Trinity, the thumb standing for the

United Godhead, and the three fingers for the separate Persons Who form It.

Beliefs concerning the mystic power of the third finger linger in country places. A gentleman to whom the writer was talking the other day said that as a little boy in Berkshire he was told to always rub ointment or lotion on a hurt with the third finger, while in Somerset you will meet folk who declare they have cured boils by rubbing them with that finger when no other had any power.

FIRE (Mascots to Prevent Destruction by)

See Bun, Cat, Wheel Cross, Houseleek, S., and Stork.

FIR TREE

A picture of a fir tree is a powerful mascot according to the Chinese who frequently use such pictures as gifts to departing friends. Probably the belief is connected with that of the influence of the pine cone (which see) though the fact that the fir is an evergreen, therefore an emblem of eternity, or at least of lasting affection, counts also.

FISH

Little fish in gold or silver or mother-of-pearl are common in almost all jeweller's, and ever since the days of the Egyptians there has been the idea that these fish mascots are particularly fortunate to lovers, and are one of the most lucky gifts sweethearts can make to each other.

This is particularly the case with those born under one of the "watery" signs of the Zodiac, as Aquarius or Pisces.

The Greeks and Romans held that the fish mascot had power to bring good luck in all affairs connected with courtship or marriage, for in the early religions the goddess of love was closely connected with water. Venus was said to have sprung from the foam of the sea, while Hathos, her Egyptian counterpart, was the Guardian of the Nile and controlled its yearly rising.

When the fish mascot happened to be a carp it was given the power of bestowing perseverance and good fortune in worldly affairs as well as bringing luck to lovers.

This is founded on an Egyptian legend that of all fish

the carp alone had courage and perseverance to leap the waterfalls and so gain the chariot of cloud which carried him to heaven.

It may be this belief was the origin of the custom of keeping gold fish—which are golden carp—as pets, though oddly enough, in some parts of England the keeping of them is considered unlucky. If one may venture a guess it might be suggested that this superstition was introduced as a reaction against the older belief. Even to-day the people of Japan hold the gold fish in veneration—it is one of the emblems of Buddha—it behoved the Christians to show their contempt for the creature. The idea grew till it came to be said that ill luck followed the fish.

FISHERMEN (Special Mascot for)
See Emerald.

FOOD LEFT ON TABLE
In some parts of the country people will exclaim in horror if the supper cloth is left on the table all night with any crumbs upon it, but apparently that tradition arose to contradict the belief in fairies and to inculcate neatness and thrift.

The older belief taught that if food were left on the table through the night, the " little people," *i.e.*, the fairies, would take it as an offering to themselves, and see that good fortune came to the house as a return.

This leaving of food in readiness for supernatural guests was particularly important on New Year's Eve, and on the eve of those days which were marked as unlucky in the calendar (see under Days).

FOOTPRINTS
Many mascots engraved to represent the imprint of a human foot are to be found in the East, and in the form illustrated is one of the " Eight Glorious Emblems "; thus, such a talisman brings the blessing of Buddha on its wearer.

Legends connected with footprints are found all over the world. For instance, there is that on Adam's Peak in Ceylon, which is visited by pilgrims of many varied creeds, who hail it respectively as the footprints of Buddha, of Mohammed, or of one or other of the Hindu gods.

In England, too, there are many " footsteps," a cele-brated case being that Field of the Forty Footsteps, whose site is covered by part of Bloomsbury. Un-fortunately all trace of the origin of the name seems to have been lost, but Southey told how he went to view the place and found he could trace not forty but seventy-six footprints. " The steps are the size of a large human foot about three inches deep and lie nearly from north-east to south-west," he says, and

FOOTPRINTS OF BUDDHA *

then adds he is quite convinced of the truth of the tradition that they were indestructible. Even though the ground had been ploughed and harrowed the footsteps appeared again.

Joseph Moser, in his " Commonplace Book," writes under date June 16, 1800 :—" Went into the fields at the back of Montague House and there saw for the last time the forty footsteps. The building materials are there, ready to cover them from the sight of man."

FORTUNA

A very powerful goddess amongst the ancients, from whose Latin name we get our words " fortune" and " fortunate." In Greece she was called Tyche. From her were derived riches and poverty, pleasures and mis-fortunes, blessings and pain. Always she was shown as a changeable goddess, but one who, on the whole, was more kindly to women than to men, and who had a special power of securing a wife the affections of her husband. Therefore, in a sense, images or portraits of her were mascots in the truest sense to all married people and to gamblers—for is not marriage a gamble?

* Reprinted by kind permission of William Rider & Son, Ltd., from the " Book of Talismans," by W. T. and K. Pavitt.

In the older sculpture she is depicted with a wheel—
symbol of change to denote her mutability, a rudder showing her guiding power, a globe to represent her world-
wide influence, and a cornucopea to stand for the prosperity it is in her power to bestow. (See Frontispiece.)
In later monuments she appears blindfolded, and sometimes winged.

FOX

Charms made in the likeness of foxes bring success in
business, perhaps because they may give the cunning of a
fox to their possessor.

FOXGLOVE

This is a mascot to those who grow it in their gardens,
providing it springs from seed, but to transplant a foxglove is unlucky. Probably its beneficent power comes
from the fairies, whose special flower it is. The gipsies
say that when a foxglove bows its head it is a certain
sign a fairy is passing by. Its old name, Many Ellyllyn,
meaning "Good People's Glove" is another link with the
fairy folk.

FRIENDSHIP (Mascots to Secure)

See Love.

FROG

Small frogs in gold or gilt metal are amulets against illness, or may be worn to hasten recovery from disease or
injury, or to win love and friendship.

That the sages of that far distant time when Ancient
Egypt was young, proclaimed the frog a sacred symbol,
shows how they founded their teachings on the wonders
of nature. They had watched the floating masses of
jelly-like substance which are the eggs of frogs, they had
seen the tiny specks within the clearness, wake to life
and hatch out as tadpoles—legless, gill-breathing creatures
that are fish to all intents and purposes. Then came the
withering of the gills, the development of lungs, the
growth of legs, until the whole of that most marvellous
metamorphosis was complete, and the frog breathed and
walked on land.

The enormous number of eggs laid by a single frog
impressed the watchers. Thus they came to regard the

creature as the symbol of Abundance or of Fertility, and in its development they saw the growth of strength out of weakness. Recovery from illness to health was typified. The remarkable length of life frogs attain was noted, as was their power to remain dormant for long periods, frequently buried away from light or air, and then able to awake apparently none the worse for their experience.

This strengthened the belief in Eternal life, in the rising from the tomb, and seeing how the frog began as a speck in floating jelly and by many changes attained his full growth, they saw in him also the symbol of the Creation, of the growth of life on the world, a teaching curiously at one with that of our most advanced thinkers. He was sacred to Ptah, the most ancient of their gods, the Beginner, the Creator of everything.

In Rome the belief in the frog mascot survived, but he was dedicated to Venus, because of his fertility, and also from the fact that in a sense he is born from foam on the water as Venus herself had been. Thus Pliny tells us that the wearing of a frog charm has power to keep love and to attract friends.

FU-KU-RO-KU-JIU

The Japanese god of Fortune and of Wisdom, whose image confers on its owner the good he represents.

GAMBLERS (Special Mascots for)

See Badger, Cat's Eye, Fortuna, Jade, Tiger, and Tooth.

GANESA

See Elephant.

GARNET

The birthstone of Virgo, but one that must be avoided by all born under Taurus. As it ensures constancy it is a favourite keepsake between parting friends, and is a very suitable stone to appear in an engagement ring.

To this familiar jewel the name Cape Ruby is given, though the true ruby is a much harder stone and the colour is more deep and rich than that of the garnet. Generally, garnets are wine red but some are so pale as to be almost a pink, while others have a decidedly

yellowish tinge.   No stone is more popular in the East
as a talisman, and in ancient Greece and Rome garnets
were favourite ornaments when engraved with portraits
of the Emperors—many of these stones are in our
museums.

In Persia the garnet is worn as a protection against
lightning, also as an antidote to the infection of plague
or fever.   In the Middle Ages it was a charm against all
diseases in which inflammation plays a part.   It has the
power of giving its wears constancy and cheerfulness so
long as possession of it is gained by legitimate means, but
a garnet which has been obtained unlawfully, carries a
curse which will fall heavily on all who possess it, until
it is returned to its rightful owner.

GARDENERS (Special Mascots for)

See Agate, Cat, and Ceres.

GEMMEL RINGS

See Rings.

GEMINI

See Zodiac.

GLOVES

From the time of their earliest introduction, gloves
have been taken as representing the hands they were made
to cover and were given a high place of honour amongst
articles of clothing.   Bishop Percy, in his " Anecdotes of
Fashion," tells that Charlemagne, about the year 790,
granted unlimited rights of hunting to the Abbot of Sithin
in order that gloves might be made of the skin of the
deer he killed.   And Stowe recounts how Edward Vere,
Earl of Oxford, after his travels on the Continent,
brought Queen Elizabeth a pair of embroidered gloves,
the first ever seen in England.

GLOVES AS GIFTS

Gloves became frequent gifts between friends and
lovers.   To give a glove was representative of offering the
hand in friendship—therefore it became a mascot—just
as throwing down a glove was a challenge to fight, or
biting the thumb of a glove was an invitation to
quarrel.

In our grandmothers' days a " young lady " was taught

the only presents she might accept from a man were gloves or flowers, and even now if a woman makes a bet with a man it frequently happens the wager is for gloves —until a few years ago no other stake was thought of where a lady was concerned.

GLOVES AND STOLEN KISSES

A writer in " The Antiquary " a few years ago asked what was the connection between gloves and forfeits for stolen kisses, but no one seemed able to answer, thus no explanation is forthcoming of the queer custom which gives a pair of gloves to the girl who sees a man asleep and kisses him before he can wake.

GLOVES, KISSES AND A NEW MOON

A far less commonly known custom is that of kissing for gloves at the new moon, which is described by Hone in his " Everyday Book " :—

"'The person in a company, male or female, who first gets a glimpse of the new moon, immediately kisses some member of the company and pronounces with a triumphant chuckle : ' Ah, Jane (or whatever her name may be) there's a pair of gloves for me ! ' '"

The same book contains an account of the use of gloves as a challenge which varies somewhat from the usual plan of casting down the gauntlet.

" On a certain Sunday, Mr Gilpin, going to preach in these parts [the Highlands] where deadly feuds prevailed, observed a glove hanging high up in the church. He demanded of the sexton what it was and why it hung there. The sexton answered that it was a glove which one in the parish hung up there as a challenge to his enemy, signifying thereby that he was ready to enter into combat hand to hand with him or with anyone else who would dare to take the glove down."

In these days we may take the gift of gloves as a sign of friendship if not of actual love, so gloves are mascots in the best sense, bringing good fortune and pleasant thoughts.

GOAT

See Capricorn, under Zodiac.

GOLD

Since the dawn of history gold has been the most valued of metals, not so much on account of its rarity as because of its beauty, and the fact that it was dedicated to Osiris in his character of the Sun.

For the latter reason it is the special metal of those born under Leo, of which sign the Sun is the ruling planet.

GOLDFISH

See Fish.

GOLLIWOG

No traditions attach to this queer creature. He is a modern invention, put on the market as a toy for children and adopted as a mascot by those who appreciate anything quaint in its ugliness.

GOOSE

Domestic happiness is secured by a talisman in the shape of a goose, according to the Chinese.

GRASSHOPPER

See Cricket.

HAMMER

In Japan hammer-shaped mascots bring success in money matters for these represent the hammer—or practically the sceptre, the sign of power—carried by Daikoku the god of wealth. See Tau Cross.

HAND

Travellers in Egypt and the Near East have brought home many little charms in the shape of hands, and it is curious to see how various are the patterns after which these hands are made, particularly with regard to the position of the fingers.

THE HAND OF LADY FATIMA

The most common is the form showing the hand with its thumb and fingers outstretched. This is a Mohammedan charm, called the Hand of Lady Fatima, from the favourite daughter of the Prophet, one of the only three women who were worthy to enter heaven.

Taken as a whole this hand represents the Holy Family of the Mussulman faith—the Prophet being symbolised by the thumb, and his daughter, Fatima, by the first finger. The middle finger is Ali, her husband, and the others her two sons.

But, in addition, the four fingers stand for Generosity, Hospitality, Power and Divine Goodness, while finally the hand reminds all true believers of the five rules of virtuous life—to keep the Fast of Ramadan, to make the Pilgrimage to Mecca, to give help to the needy, to perform the necessary ablutions, and to fight against the Infidel.

HAND OF FATIMA *

THE SIGN OF BENEDICTION

The hand with the third and fourth fingers and the thumb closed, the first and second fingers being outstretched, is the sacred sign of Benediction in the Christian Churches.

THE DEVIL'S HORN

When the hand is clenched with the first and fourth fingers outstretched, it is called the Devil's Horn in Italy, though it is used as a mascot for all that. Probably it is a form of the horns or crescent of Isis, and, in the Christian reaction against the older faith, the present uncomplimentary name was given.

AGAINST THE EVIL EYE

A clenched hand with all the fingers closed and the thumb between the first and second, is a common amulet in Etruscan tombs, while a clenched hand with the first finger extended—exactly as we see on our guide posts— is found in Greece as a charm against the Evil Eye. In most cases these mascots are made of blue glass, though metal ones painted or enamelled blue are seen occasionally.

PALM OF HAND

A favourite Japanese mascot is the imprint of a child's hand on a sheet of paper. The little one's palm is

* Reprinted by kind permission of William Rider & Son, Ltd., from the " Book of Talismans," by W. T. and K. Pavitt.

covered with ink and pressed on the sheet, which is afterwards pasted on the wall of the house to ward off evil influences. See also Finger.

HARE

Strictly speaking no mention of the hare should be made in any list of modern mascots. He is a luck bringer indeed, but a bringer of bad luck. Burton, in his "Anatomy of Melancholy," refers to this belief by saying "There is a fear which is commonly caused by prodigies which much trouble many of us, as if a hare cross our way at our going forth."

Yet the Druids used the hare for purposes of divination, and when Boadicea went into battle against the Romans she carried a hare in her breast as a luck bringer. It is possible that her defeat may have been the reason why the hare obtained the reputation of being unlucky.

The gipsies say even hare's foot clover must never be gathered. The ill fortune of the name clings to it.

HARP

A form of the lyre, the symbol of Apollo, the harp stands for all that is elevating in art and music. A mascot in the truest and most beautiful sense.

HANUMAN

The monkey god of the Hindus, the giver of good fortune of very kind, has special power against the Evil Eye.

HAWK

To an extent the hawk seems to have been confused with the eagle, for in Egyptian mythology both are connected with the sun. The bird was sacred to Horus, and through him had influence with Isis. A general bringer of good luck, of light coming when darkness seems at hand.

HAWTHORN

A bough of hawthorn fastened outside the house door will bring good fortune to those within, according to a very ancient belief, but on no account must it be brought over the threshold. To have any part of hawthorn indoors, but particularly the flowers, is to court disaster. Yet it is a fortunate tree to have in the garden.

HEART

Mascots shaped as hearts are given as signs of love or friendship, and typify the expression of " giving a heart " as meaning the bestowing of affection. In ancient Egypt talismans in heart form were guards against black magic.

The heart played an important part in Egyptian religion. It was taught that at the Judgment the hearts of the dead were weighed, and those found good were returned to their original owners, who thereupon literally rose from the grave, perfect in all respects. For those whose hearts were bad there was no resurrection.

HEATHER

That a sprig of white heather is a mascot to protect from danger and to grant any wish that is persistently desired, is a widespread belief, probably originating in the fact that natural white heather is very rare. A man might walk for many miles over purple heather without seeing a single white bell, but if his eye did happen to light on one while a wish was in his mind, then that wish " would come true." It may be, however, that there is some deeper and more occult lore underlying the belief, a lore that has been forgotten. We know the Celts used heather in their ceremonies and divinations, and at least two Scottish clans (the Macdonalds and the Macdougals) claim the heather, in different forms, as their badges.

The Macpherson legends of Ossian associate white heather with tears, but Macpherson must not be accepted implicitly. According to him, when Oscar, son of Ossian, lay dying in Ulster after his fight with Cairbar, he gave one of his followers a sprig of purple heather, bidding the man take it to his sweetheart, Malvina, as a token that his last thoughts were hers—perhaps also as a sign of the immortality of his love. The man obeyed, and when Malvina received the message her tears fell so bitterly on the sprig of heather that its flowers grew white, and ever since white heather has been a symbol of her faithful love. The likeness of the story to that of Baldr and Nanna (see Mistletoe) cannot be overlooked.

HOLLY

A mascot which brings prosperity and general good fortune to a house, particularly at Christmas time, but it is important that Christmas decorations must not be removed until the New Year at least—in some parts of the country they are never disturbed until Candlemas Day (February 2nd). For the legend of the holly see Mistletoe.

HORN

Always a mascot bringing good fortune and prosperity, and having power to combat the influence of the evil eye.

ANTELOPE'S HORN

A mascot much worn in Italy to avert every form of evil.

COW'S HORN

In many parts of the country cow's horns are found hanging at the doors of the byres, and if farmers are asked why the horns are there, the reply will probably be that, "It's a bit of old foolishness," and no one has thought about any reason. Their fathers always had horns near the byres, and so did their fathers before them, so the custom has grown.

But originally those horns were offerings to Isis, an entreaty that she, the mother goddess, would help the cows when they came to calve, and grant a plentiful supply of milk afterwards.

See also Crescent and Cornucopea.

HIPPOPOTAMUS

In old Egypt the hippopotamus was the symbol of Ta-urt, the goddess who held the key to Divine wisdom and to human reason. Thus, as a mascot, the hippopotamus brings far-reaching knowledge and great understanding. See Sa.

HORSESHOE

In the first instance the horseshoe was regarded as a bringer of good luck because of its likeness to a crescent, the symbol of Isis. But in addition it was credited with special virtue because it was made of iron—a metal that had power over the Evil Eye.

The Greeks and Romans nailed horseshoes against

their walls as safeguard against plague, taking care the shoes were hung with the horns upward. Practically all over the world will be found the same idea. The explanation given of the position is generally that if turned the other way round "the luck will run out," though another version has it that the bad luck is trapped in the circle and as the devil cannot cross the opening he will keep running backwards and forwards inside.

When used in conjunction with the wood of the ash tree the horseshoe was an important medicinal charm in the Middle Ages. Frequently a shoe was buried in the roots of an ash, or sometimes it was hung on an ash bough, so that in course of time the wood grew round it. In either case a twig from the tree thus treated had only to be draw over the backs of cattle and they were cured of all ills.

In Bermuda it is the custom to thrust a horseshoe into the fire if any suspected witch or known enemy is approaching the house, in the belief that the iron takes greater power when wedded to heat.

In the depths of our mines it is quite common to see horseshoes nailed to the sides of the workings, and on the east coast, but particularly in Suffolk, fishermen nail horeshoes to the masts of their boats.

"May the horseshoe never be pulled from your threshold," is a good wish quoted in the very old play, "The Marriage of the Arts," by Holiday.

In Hudibras there is the mention of a conjurer who drove away evil spirits with horeshoes and sickles—both forms of the crescent. Gay in his fable, "The Old Woman and Her Cats," tells how the witch is worried by straws laid across over which she cannot pass—another form of the charm of the cross—and by the horseshoes which guard doorways.

Brand tells us that in Monmouth Street, London, he counted no less than seventeen horseshoes nailed against the steps of the houses, but going there again thirty years later (1846) he could only find five or six.

He quotes from Aubrey's "Miscellanies":—"Under the porch of Staninfield Church in Suffolk I saw a tile with a horseshoe on it, placed there for this purpose [to drive away witches], though one would imagine the holy water alone would have been sufficient. I am told there are many similar instances."

In China alone the horseshoe is not a popular mascot, but there the hoof of a horse is accounted a great luck bringer.

HORSE

In the North of England, wherever the influence of the Danes lingers, a horse is looked upon as a true mascot, a bringer of good fortune, because of its association with Sleipner, the eight-footed horse which belonged to Odin, and amongst the Greeks, Pegasus, the winged steed, was a mascot, lifting the soul to the heights of beauty and love. In both these cases the horse represented swiftness of thought, strength and devotion, therefore he stood for good.

PIEBALD HORSE

There is a common belief that if anyone happens to be wishing deeply for some object, and at that moment meets a piebald horse face to face, the wish will be granted, just as the wish is doomed to disappointment if the animal's tail is seen. No reason for this belief can be discovered : probably it arose because piebald horses are comparatively rare.

WHITE HORSE

In spite of what has been said of the horse as a mascot, in the Midlands and the Southern counties you will be told you should always spit, preferably over the left shoulder, should you meet a white horse face to face. The reason for this is not far to seek. All the Southern part of England and much of the Midlands as well, was laid waste by the Saxon hordes who poured into the country under the banner emblazoned with the sign of the White Horse, hence white horses are associated with rapine and murder in the popular mind. In the same way it is said that the ghost of either Hengist or Horsa, the Saxon leaders, haunts the lanes of Kent in the shape of a giant white horse, a further reason for connecting the animal with evil.

SEA HORSE

In Italy, little models of sea horses are frequently worn as protection against the Evil Eye, and the creatures are shown in many of the Pompeian paintings. They had been placed upon the walls of the houses to avert ill fortune from those within.

HOTEI

The children's deity of Japan may be identified—at least to a great extent—with Bes. He is shown as a stout, comfortable-looking being sitting on a bag of good things —surely a first cousin to the sack which Santa Claus brings down the chimney from his reindeer sledge.

HOUSELEEK

This little plant was encouraged to grow on thatched roofs from the belief that its presence would save the house from destruction by fire. The writer knew an old lady in Dorset who used to gather houseleek and hang a bit by her chimney with her kettle-holder. When questioned she had no idea why she did it, she had seen it done sometime and thought it was lucky. Probably it was another form of the charm against fire.

HUNTERS (Special Mascot for)

See Amethyst.

INDRA'S THUNDERBOLT

An important Hindu talisman, may be roughly described as two arrow heads or darts each surrounded by a cord. It is carried to avert the influence of demons and to secure good fortune, representing the thunderbolts of Indra, the god of the weather, who gives rain to the parched lands and fights the demon of drought.

IRON

INDRA'S   The metal of those born under Scorpio.
THUNDERBOLT *   Iron was first discovered and worked by the Hindus, for its manufacture was carried on in the East while the peoples of Europe used bronze. To Greece the use of iron was introduced slowly, but when the

* Reprinted by kind permission of William Rider & Son, Ltd., from the " Book of Talismans," by W. T. and K. Pavitt.

Romans conquered Britain they were astonished to find the inhabitants were skilled in the manufacture of iron—proof of the advanced civilisation of the Britons.

Being dug as " earth " it is natural that iron should be specially identified with all who work in connection with the soil—farmers, ploughmen, engineers, metal craftsmen and miners, all look on iron as their mascot. Again, it forms the most important talismans against all evil spirits—the good that comes out of the ground fighting the evil that lurks in the depths.

JACINTH

As a birth stone, belongs to Aquarius, but to ensure it exercising its full power it must be set in gold. To those born under Taurus or Scorpio it will bring ill luck.

This is another name for a zircon, being given to stones which are deep orange or bright red in colour. It was a very popular charm in the Middle Ages, as it had medicinal powers which would stimulate the appetite of its wearer, cure indigestion, and protect from fever, plague or dropsy. It was popular with travellers also, as it was claimed to have power against robbers. In India it is much worn as an antidote against poison.

JADE

The birth stone of those born under Virgo, but must be avoided by Sagittarius or Gemini people. It is a gambler's mascot, and gives success in any game of chance, but especially in connection with racing.

The brilliant green colour of this stone is well known; indeed it has given its name to the particular dye, and all over the world carved beads of jade are worn as talismans.

In China some of the finest jade is found, and there, from the dawn of history, charms in the shape of bats or storks carved in jade have been worn to ensure long life. Probably because of its colour it shares with the emerald the reputation of being a charm against troubles of the eye, and from ancient times right through the Middle Ages it was a recognised remedy for all kidney and digestive ills. In this connection lies a point of great interest.

When the explorers from the East sailed for the new land of the West and discovered Central America, they found the natives wearing jade ornaments—much jade is found in Peru—and learnt that these ornaments were worn as charms against kidney disease and stone in the bladder!

Also, jade is the " green stone " of New Zealand. It is used to make the blades of the ceremonial axes which are carried as sceptres by the chiefs of New Caledonia, and formed the heads of the clubs called " mere " made for the use of Maoris of the highest rank. Generally the chiefs devoted these particular weapons to the killing of prisoners.

JASPER

See Bloodstone.

JET

Belongs to Saturn as a birth stone, and must be avoided by the people of Libra and Aries, also by all young people, as Saturn is never favourable to the young. Providing their birth dates are favourable it is the special mascot of travellers, and a great charm against witchcraft.

In the Middle Ages jet was called Black Amber, and mascots carved of it were in great demand as charms against fits, while in his description of the British Isles Henry of Huntingdon tells us that :—" Britain furnished large quantities of very excellent jet of a black and brilliant hue. Rendered sparkling by fire it drives away serpents; when it is heated by friction, substances adhere to it as they do to amber."

The Greeks dedicated jet to the goddess Cybele, who presided over all the things which spring from the earth.

JOCHEBED

This name of the mother of Moses is a powerful Eastern talisman if written on a small scroll and tied round the neck. It saves from the evil eye, while if repeated aloud many times it forms a charm by which lost things are found and secrets revealed.

JUROJIN

The Japanese god of health. He can banish disease, cure illness, prevent infection, and lengthen life.

KEY

As a modern mascot the key is given and accepted as a sign of love—symbolical of locking or unlocking the door of the heart.

GREEK KEY OF LIFE

In ancient Greece and Rome the single key was the most important of all mascots, as perhaps it was the oldest, dating from the most remote antiquity. Possibly it is even older than the Swastika.

It was the Key of Life and also the Key of the Door though which the prayers of the devout reached the gods, thus these key talismans were made in silver—the metal of Diana—because Diana, under her name of Jana, was joint custodian of the Doorway with Janus, though she specially presided over the threshold. It will be remembered she was the guardian of child-bearing women, and thus watched over the threshold of life.

The key mascot opened the door by which prayers reached the gods; it was the symbol of the entrance to life, and as a talisman was worn to promote Remembrance of Things Past and Foresight for Things to Come.

Often these keys were attached to little heart-shaped handles when they became the symbols of guarded affection.

THREE KEYS *

THREE KEYS

These form a common Japanese mascot, and are worn to unlock the doors leading to Love, Health and Wealth.

THE KEY OF HECATE

Silver keys attached to finger rings were those of Hecate, goddess of the underworld, who had power over the spirits of the departed. Such a key formed a link between the

* Reprinted by kind permission of William Rider & Son, Ltd., from the "Book of Talismans," by W. T. and K. Pavitt.

living and the dead. It was another form of the Key of the Door.

THE KEY TO BANISH BAD DREAMS

Gipsies say that if you hang a door key upside-down near your bed you will be safe from all forms of evil, and secure good repose. Probably this is a charm against Mare, the evil spirit of the night, the bringer of bad dreams, from whom we get the word "nightmare." A ring of any kind, but particularly of iron or stone, was the talisman against her visits, thus in this case the ring at the top of the key would hold the charm.

KNIVES

The commonest of all popular beliefs is surely that which declares knives and scissors and brooches (because of the sharp pins) are unlucky as gifts, therefore must be bought, even though the price paid is the smallest coin possible. In some places it is added that though the gift of a knife or other cutting instrument is unlucky at any time, it is doubly so at Easter.

Yet all along the East Coast you will hear old women say that if a knife is found in a baby's cradle it will bring the child good luck, and not so very long ago a knife was always placed in the first cradle in which a new-born child was laid.

Our East Coast is closely associated with Denmark, many of the words in the local dialects are the same, and Danish customs and Danish ways of thought are everywhere. This belief is a case in point. In old Denmark, when a child was about to be born, a bag containing rosemary, salt, bread and a knife was hung over the cradle prepared for the little one's reception.

Yet a knife was not always thought unlucky as a gift, for knives were common presents for groomsmen to give brides in the Middle Ages, when the bride invariably carried a knife at her wedding as the brides of to-day carry bouquets. The idea was that the knife would cut the bridegroom's love if it were not true, but would be powerless so long as he gave her his devotion.

A knife falling on the floor is a sign that a visitor may be expected, according to an old story whose origin is difficult to trace, but the other common knife belief—that crossed knives foretell a quarrel—is easy of explanation. In the days when men went armed, a quarrel and a fight were pretty much the same thing, and in fights knives were crossed with a vengeance.

KNOTS

The knot is the symbol of lasting love, of a troth that is plighted for all eternity.

Yet in another sense a knot is a hindrance. All over the country you will hear it said that if a woman in labour wears any garment tied with a knotted string her child cannot be born, and if a person lies dying, care must be taken nothing tied with a knot is near. The writer remembers seeing a valance untied from a deathbed, and taken away because it was fastened to the bedstead by tapes that were tied in knots.

TRUE LOVERS' KNOT

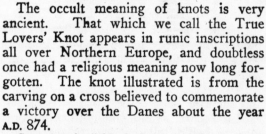

The occult meaning of knots is very ancient. That which we call the True Lovers' Knot appears in runic inscriptions all over Northern Europe, and doubtless once had a religious meaning now long forgotten. The knot illustrated is from the carving on a cross believed to commemorate a victory over the Danes about the year A.D. 874.

Some authorities believe the knot on the runes is a distorted form of the rod of Mercury, and indeed very little imagination is needed to trace a likeness between the two.

RUNIC KNOT

THE KNOT IN LOVE SPELLS

Gay, in his Pastoral, "The Spell," describes how a country girl, seeing a lad sleeping by the roadside, managed to steal his garter. This she tied with her own into a true lovers' knot, thus working a spell which held his love to her forever. She says :—

Three times a true-love's knot I tie secure :
Firm be the knot, firm may his love endure.

Brand quotes from a publication called " The Connoisseur," which gives the following charm :—

" Whenever I go to lye in a strange bed I always tye my garter nine times round the bedpost and tye nine knots in it, and say to myself,

" ' This knot I tye,
This knot I tye,
To see my love as he goes bye,
In his apparel'd array
As he walks in every day.' "

Brand adds quaintly :—" This is, of course, intended for poetry."

WEDDING KNOTS

In China knots play an important part in all wedding decorations. Part of the marriage ceremony consists of the bridegroom holding a red ribbon and the bride a green one which are knotted together.

LADDER OR STEPS

Charms made in this shape date from ancient Egypt, though the ladder has played an important part in all religious teachings. The Biblical story of Jacob's ladder will be remembered.

In Egypt, Horus was known as the god of the ladder, and small ladders, to be worn as personal charms, were used to secure his aid, chiefly in connection with a desire to leave behind all that was of the earth earthy and to reach the greater heights.

It was believed that heaven was an actual country placed above the earth, the sky being its floor, an idea which lingered until well into Victorian times, to say the least. The Egyptians thought a ladder was necessary to reach this higher plane, and that this ladder could be obtained only from Horus, the rising sun. According to some of the paintings in the Pyramids, there seem to have been two ladders, one on which the soul had to climb out of the darkness of the grave, and another leading upwards to the pinnacle of eternal light.

In the same way Osiris was called the god of the staircase or way by which the souls of the dead reached everlasting light. And there was a legend that when Horus was killed he descended into darkness, but returned to life by way of the ladder Osiris passed down to him.

LADYBIRDS

Among living mascots few are more popular than the familiar red ladybird, which is recognised as a luck bringer always. The usual story goes that if a ladybird settles on the hand you may expect to receive money before long, but only on condition you do not harm the little creature. The fact that the ladybird is a kind of beetle, and therefore a close connection of the sacred scarab, may have some importance.

The familiar rhyme :—

Ladybird, ladybird, fly away home,
Your house is on fire and your children will burn

is not easy to account for, but may be survival of some forgotten incantation. Probably the words we use are quite apart from those of the original version—in another language—though they have some phonetic resemblance.

LAMB

A sacred symbol, dating from very early days, to represent gentleness and sacrifice. See Agnus Dei.

LAPIS LAZULI

The birth stone of Libra, but must be avoided by all born under Cancer or Capricorn.

This is a deep blue stone, much used for engraving upon by the Ancients, and is generally supposed to have been the stone mentioned in the Bible as that on which the Tables of the Law were inscribed. The Bible gives it as sapphire, but probably that is a mistranslation. " Blue stone " was the original phrase, and the rendering " sapphire " is easily understandable.

Because of its colour it was sacred to Isis, and then to Venus, while the early Christians dedicated it to the Holy Virgin. A necklace of the blue beads was worn as a cure for apoplexy or epilepsy, also for skin troubles or poorness of the blood; it had power to raise drooping spirits, to strengthen friendship, and secure the fidelity of a lover.

The Old Masters used ground lapis lazuli as a pigment, particularly when they were portraying the robes of the Holy Virgin, and it is still employed in the preparations of the finest kinds of ultramarine.

LAUREL

The emblem of victory, of success after struggle, but a tree that is fortunate in many ways. Gipsies say that no quarrels will disturb a house which has laurel bushes around it.

LAVENDER

Perhaps because of their blue colour lavender flowers are fortunate for lovers, though lavender is a " herb of Mercury." Not so very long ago it was thought essential that an intending bride should have bags of lavender flowers amongst her trousseau in order to ensure good fortune.

LEAD

Astrologically the special metal for those born under Capricorn and Aquarius.

After copper this was probably the first metal of which man had knowledge, certainly it was used in very early times. It is mentioned in the Book of Job, when Job in his misery cries :—" Oh, that my words were now written ! . . . That they were graved with an iron pen and lead in the rock forever."

Alluding to this passage, Bishop Harmer writes :—" It has been supposed that Job alludes to letters hollowed in a rock with an iron pen or chisel and filled with molten lead in order to be more legible. The Septuagint, however, seem to have suspected he meant the recording of things by engraving them on sheets of lead."

LEAP YEAR PENNY
LEE PENNY

See Penny.

LEO

See Zodiac.

LIBRA

See Zodiac.

LIGHTNING (Mascots Which Protect From)
See Cornelian, Garnet, and Malachite.

LION

As a mascot the king of beasts gives strength and courage, especially if the mascot is made in gold or any yellow metal, and the wearer of it was born under Leo. Lions symbolise the sun, and in that connection they were represented as drawing the chariot of Cybele, goddess of all that sprang from the earth.

LIZARD

Everywhere in tradition and folk-lore and mythology, the lizard is connected with the power of sight, with light in some form or another, hence the belief that ill-fortune, probably in the form of eye trouble, will befall those who kill or injure lizards.

The emerald was the special stone of expectant mothers and the lizard had power over the unborn also. Therefore if any woman who is to become a mother, or who wishes to have a child, sees a lizard cross her path, she may look forward to happiness for herself and for the child she will surely bear.

Country folks say that a sleeper in the open will be wakened by the lizard if a poisonous snake appears.

This is another belief that can be traced to the Ancients, when, by reason of its bright green colouring, the lizard was said to be related to the emerald, the stone that gave sight to the blind—so to-day the story runs the lizard acts as eyes to the sleeping man.

In Rome the lizard was the symbol of All-Seeing Wisdom, and was the device for the shield of Minerva. Rings engraved with the figure of a lizard were worn as a charm against blindness.

Frequently the lizard was engraved on other jewels, as well as rings, and in Portugal it is a favourite decoration to paint on the walls of houses still, the idea being that it wards off ill-luck.

LODESTONE

The special talisman for sailors, and for the cure of gout. Wise women of old ordered sufferers from the complaint to wear lodestones next the skin.

As a birth stone it belongs to Scorpio, but is doubly fortunate to those born under the sign if their work is connected with iron in any form. Those born under Aquarius or Leo should avoid it.

During the Middle Ages the lodestone was frequently set in wedding rings because it had the power of winning and holding love, to be a magnet for hearts as for metals. In the East it is much worn as a charm to protect from spirits of evil, while in India it is said to give health and strength to its wearer in addition to safeguarding him from the evil eye.

LOTUS FLOWER

A talisman to ensure good health and good fortune.

Many kinds of water lily are known as lotus flowers, but the true lotus of Hindu and Chinese mythology is the Nelumbium lutem, a very beautiful lily which was regarded as the emblem of fertility in ancient Egypt, and used for the wreaths which decorated the brow of their holy Isis. In India it is one of the Glorious Emblems of Buddha. As it is used very frequently in conventional drawing it may be found on wall papers and friezes. A better design could hardly be imagined—its presence on the walls of a house should bring health and domestic happiness to those who dwell within.

LYRE

LYRE

The early form of harp with which Apollo is portrayed. As a mascot the lyre gives lofty thoughts and success in any high ambition.

LOVERS (Special Mascots to Attract Love and Friendship)

Love mascots are all connected with the influence of Venus, or her older counterpart, Hathos, in some form or another. In dealing with these mascots several charms and fragments of folk-lore have been included. See Acorn, Agate, Amethyst, Aquamarine, Andromeda, Arrow, Bangle, Beans, Beryl, Blackthorn, Bow, Bull, Cherry, Colour, Crescent, Cupid, Daikoku, Daisy, Days, Emerald, Finger, Fish, Frog, Garnet, Gloves, Heart, Key, Knot, Lapis Lazuli, Lavender, Lodestone, Marsh Mallow, Malachite, Menat, Moon, Moonstone, Myrtle, Padlock, Ring, Rosemary, Shoes, Sigil, Southernwood, Stones, Torch, Turquoise, and Vulture.

MALACHITE

The birthstone of Capricorn, and the special mascot to raise the spirits and inspire hope, especially when engraved with the figure of the sun.

Most people know this beautiful green stone only in the form of beads, but it is greatly worn in Russia and throughout the East as a protection against rheumatism, while the Hindus see in it a charm against cholera. It protects from lightning, and gives health and success and happy love.

MANDRAKE

As a mascot the root of this plant is specially powerful with women who wished to have children : in that case it should be worn hung round the neck. Also it seems the mandrake has power to grant other wishes, though it was used in sorcery and in Black Magic as a means of working harm. There was an old belief that the mandrake was endowed with human life and power of feeling pain. It might only be dragged from the ground at certain hours astrologically laid down, otherwise when touched it would scream aloud with such an awful voice that madness would fall on the daring being who disturbed it. This belief is mentioned by Shakespeare, when Juliet speaks of,

. . . shrieks, like mandrakes torn out of the earth,
That living mortals, hearing them, run mad.

MARSH MALLOWS

These familiar wayside flowers are not generally recognised as mascots, but according to a gipsy they help lovers. This is the charm that can be worked with them :

" There be marsh mallows that will cure all sorts of ill. You gather a handful of they flowers and stand they outside your door or on your window sill in a jar of water, and them there dear little flowers will draw your sweetheart along to you.

THE MENAT *

"It be a charm them work to help you, not a spell, for a charm and a spell is two different things. A charm is harmless and may do you good, but a spell be laid on you by black magic and is put on you by shovi-hauns and such evil-minded persons."

THE MENAT

An Egyptian talisman worn to promote health, and to bring happiness in love or marriage. It was specially dedicated to Hathos, the Egyptian goddess of whom it was said she stood for all that is good and true in Wife, Mother and Daughter.

MERRYTHOUGHT

The " wishbone " or " merrythought " of any fowl is a well known mascot, and its use as a luck-bringer and as a means of telling whether " wishes will come true " is a survival of some very old form of divination.

Little " merrythoughts " made in gold or silver are frequently included in bunches of charms. They give success in anything which is ardently wished for, though perhaps their virtue lies in their horseshoe-like shape.

In the " British Apollo," published in 1709, the question is asked and answered thus :—

Q.—For what reason is the bone next the breast of a fowl called the merrythought, and when was it first called so?

A.—The original of the name was doubtless from the pleasant fancies that commonly arise on the breaking of that bone and 'twas then certainly first called so when these merry fancies were first started.

MICE

But especially shrew mice, were sacred to Apollo. They were allowed to live round his altars, they were fed in

* Reprinted by kind permission of William Rider & Son, Ltd., from the " Book of Talismans," by W. T. and K. Pavitt.

his holy of holies, and the image of a mouse was placed beside his sacred tripod. In many cities of Egypt mice and rats were worshipped, probably because they were early totems (see Totem) of the prehistoric tribes. Herodotus, however, tells that when Sennacherib invaded Egypt, the Egyptian king Sethos was without an army and almost in despair, when in a dream he was told he would be saved by divine intervention. That night the invaders slept on the field, and when morning broke it was discovered field mice had gnawed their quivers and their shield bands, so that they were practically at the mercy of those they had come to kill. A statue was raised of Sethos, showing him with a mouse in his hand.

MINERS (Special Mascot for)

See Iron and Horseshoe.

MISTLETOE

Mistletoe is the beneficent plant to lovers, though it must never be carried into any sacred building and is not used in church decorations. This is traceable to the legend of the mistletoe's part in the death of Baldr, as told in Norse mythology.

Baldr, the white god, incurred the hatred of Utgarde Loki, who formed an arrow out of the mistletoe with which to kill the god. In the course of some game, Baldr paused beside a bush, when the fatal arrow sped on its way, and found its mark—his heart—in spite of the warning sent by Odin's war bird, the cock. The white god fell dying, but because the bush by which he stood had tried to shelter him, Odin ordered henceforward it should never die but become an evergreen and bear red berries in memory of Baldr's blood being spilt on it. That is our holly. The mistletoe became accursed because of the arrow, yet the tears of Nanna, Baldr's wife, fell upon it and became pearls. Thus for her sake the mistletoe was dedicated to women who love, though it was banished from the presence of the gods. The Fathers of the Christian Church were too wise to combat old beliefs, rather they grafted their own teachings on to them. Thus the holly which had sheltered the dying god was used in the decoration of Christian churches, while the mistletoe was forbidden to be brought with the sacred buildings, just as it had been taboo from the temples of the Norsemen's gods.

MITSU-DOMOE

A very curious Japanese talisman, worn as protection from fire, flood or theft. It is in the form of a circle, enclosing three strange figures which remotely resemble fish, and represent the elements, Fire, Air and Water.

MOLES

That moles—which are birthmarks and must not be confused with freckles—have some sort of bearing on the fortune of the person on whom they appear, is a very old belief, and had its foundation in astrology. Each mole was said to have this or that meaning according to its colour and the part of the body on which it is placed, since astrologically certain planets—*i.e.*, certain influences—rule particular limbs and organs.

The astrologer, Richard Sanders, who lived in the seventeenth century, was a great authority on moles, and it is possible, though not certain, that he was the first to advance the theory that when a mole appears on any part of the body, another is invariably to be found on a certain position on the face to balance it. He says :— "From moles on the face we find other moles on the body and derive a certain judgment therefrom."

The study of moles had fallen into the ranks of almost forgotten superstitions, until a few years ago when a well known explorer openly declared his faith in it and actually wrote a book on the subject, dedicating it to a very popular dramatist, who shared his belief in what he cleverly calls " Moleosophy."

To quote from that book—which deals in a most exhaustive manner with the meanings of moles, though it gives no attempt at explanation of the means of deduction used, nor of the history of the science—would not be possible here. However the following is taken from an old " chap book," a queer little production, printed on greyish paper, full of interest from many points of view, though unfortunately the greater part of its contents is unfit for modern publication. Here is its information regarding moles, literally transcribed except for a few necessary omissions.

DREAMS & Moles

with

Their Interpretation & Signification

made far more manifest & plain than any published to the meanest capacities, by the most Ancient as well as the most modern Rules of Philosophy.

to which is Added

A Collection of choice & Valuable

Receipts

concerning

Love & Marriage

Printed & sold by G. Thompson, 48 Love Lane, Smithfield.

OF MOLES.

It is confessed by most modern authors, that as the wise archetect of this spacious globe thought fit most graciously in his own image to make him the sole ruler on earth, so he imprinted on man many marks of history, that thereby he might read some of the events which will befal him in the series of his life. Now these historical marks are no more than spots in the flesh, commonly called moles, which as their situation is various, so they differ much in nature and quality; some are black, others grey, some are red, having a small lock of hair spreading out. The situation being the basis on which will befal us. Wherefore I could wish my tender reader not to be angry at a mole which my book bespeaks ominous; nor on the other hand let him flatter himself when it shows fair.

" So sure as Dame Fortune's wheel turns round,
He that's born to be hanged will never be drowned.

OF MOLES IN GENERAL. Their Origin, Colour, Nature, and Situation in either Sex—With Their true Signification, and how far they extend to the good and bad fortune of mankind.

If a mole is on the crown of the head, it shows another on the nape of the neck, and the party witty, and to have good natural parts, but that he will die poor.

One on the middle of the forehead shows a man industrious and a woman very fruitful.

A woman having a mole on her chin will have a long clack.

He that has one on his left cheek, line of Mercury, threatens crosses, and imprisonment.

He that has one on the upper lip will have exceeding good fortune; but a woman will be debauched.

Moles on both side of the neck, opposite each other, threaten the person with loss of life.

The left side of the throat shows the party is to suffer much by bruises, if it happens on a man; but if on a woman, it shows her much in danger by water.

A mole on the right arm of a man shows that he is given to gaming, but to a woman riches from her parents, and to gain the esteem of the world.

A mole between the elbow and the wrist; on the left wrist shows crosses in their issue, but to obtain great wealth.

A mole with one black hair shows the party:

"Shall unto poetry bend his mind
And with the world acceptance find
Much of divinity he'll write,
And strive to improve it day and night.
A traveller he will be, in hope,
To see his holiness the Pope;
Not much of fortune's smiles he'll have,
Nor will he much for honour crave;
He'll liberal be, and one who will
Strive to do nothing that is ill.
All the vexations of his life,
Will be in chosing of a wife;
Nothing shall more him ever entice,
His footsteps in the paths of vice.
I cannot think on earth he'll have,
One foot of land to dig a grave;
But surely he at sea shall die,
And in some watery tomb shall lie.

If a mole appears on the back, it denotes much riches by means of very great persons.

A mole on the upper part of the left side of the back
shows long journeys, and imprisonment to a man; and to
a woman that she may travel to some far distant land.

One on the left side of the breast, shows very bad fortune to a man, by displeasing his superiors; to a woman
poverty by means of neglect.

> " That person will be much inclined,
> Unto a sad debauched Mind;
> Never till drunk he'll be at rest,
> Who hath a mole on his left breast.
> The man to game will be inclined,
> The woman of a frantic mind;
> The man no quiet day shall see,
> By reason of debauchery;
> Nor the woman proove a quiet wife,
> During the term of all her life.

A mole on the right side of the shoulder blade, shows a
person firm in his resolutions and of a very healthy con-
stitution; and to a woman it signifies great success.

> " Thus have I finished what I knew
> Concerning moles, which I've found true;
> For moles that on our bodies grow,
> Do promise either bliss or woe;
> Not that I'd have you trust so far;
> To throw aside all worldly care;
> Many do this when heaven above,
> His wished for joys can soon remove.
> Therefore let not the reader's faith,
> Depend on what the author saith;
> Nor pin it on a rotten sleeve,
> Lest disappointment he receive."

While on the subject, Brand may be quoted also. It is
not without interest to compare his information with that
of the writer of the chap book.

This, from his " Antiquities," is very slightly altered
in deference to modern ideas.

" Misson, in his Travels in England, translated by
Ozell, observed, p. 583, that ' when Englishmen, *i.e.*, the
common people, have warts or moles on their faces, they
are very careful of the great hairs that grow out of these

excrescences; and several have told me they look on these hairs as tokens of good luck.'

" The following on this most ridiculous subject is preserved in the Twelfth Book of A Thousand Notable Things: ' (9) A mole on the feet and hands (sic) denotes many children. (10) Moles on the arms and shoulders denote great wisdom; on the left, debate and contention. Moles near the armhole, riches and honour. A mole on the neck commonly denotes one on the stomach, which denotes strength. (11) A mole on the neck and throat denotes riches and health. A mole on the chin, another near the heart, and signifies riches. (12) A mole on the lip signifies great talkers. (13) A mole on the right side of the forehead is a sign of great riches, both to men and women; and on the other side quite the contrary. Moles on the ankles or feet denote courage in men and modesty in women. A mole on or about the knee signifies riches and virtue; if on a woman's left knee many children. A mole on the left side of the heart denotes very ill qualities. A mole on the breast denotes poverty.' "

MONEY

See Coins and Pennies.

MONEY SWORD

An all powerful Chinese talisman to guard a house from any form of ill luck. It is formed of two iron rods, one short and one long, tied to a form a cross or sword, and then covered with the Chinese coins which are pierced by square holes so that they are easily fastened to the sword. It is important that all fastenings must be made with red silk (see under Colours), and the sword should be hung over the bed of the master of the house, pointing from right to left.

MONKEY

See Hanuman, the monkey god.

MONOGRAMME

See Sigil.

MOON

According to astrology the phase of the moon at any particular time has a special bearing on all our actions, and it is by the moon chiefly that calculations are made which declare certain days are lucky and certain unlucky. Most of the religious feasts, as, for instance, the Christian Easter and the Jewish Passover, are fixed by the moon.

A very wide-spread belief declares any new venture in love or business or art, which is begun at the time of the seventh new moon of the year, is sure to be successful.

To the worship of Isis we can trace many of the beliefs regarding the moon that linger amongst us. Particularly is this the case in the old saying that when a woman sees the new moon for the first time she should bow and turn a silver coin in her pocket—the turning of the coin being symbolical of the moon's power over the tides. In some parts of England the woman is told to bow three times—in doing so she does homage to the Egyptian Trinity, Osiris, Isis, and Horus, the Father, the Mother, the Son.

To the same religion can be traced the idea that the moon has an effect upon health in certain of her phases. In this connection it is worth while to quote the belief of the Romanys, as told to the writer by a gipsy in the New Forest :—

" 'Tis a strange thing what a wonderful great power the moon's got to control and draw human beings to her, like as her do draw the tides of the sea. You may not believe it, but some quiet-going folk as don't seem as if nothing ever moves them, goes quite queer in their minds at the turn of the moon.

" What be the turn of the moon, do you ask?

" Why, the time betwixt the old moon's fading away and the new moon's up-rising, for sure. If folks only knowed how the moon do draw the tides inside of we and raise them up out of our own control, they'd take more care of theyselves at such a time.

" Us have strong, fast-running swashways in our blood and contrary currents what will rise up of a sudden and threaten to destroy everything, 'specially if us be of mixed blood. Then that of the Romany will clash with the other and will raise great waves in us like when the tide comes in against the wind. Turn of the moon and full of the moon—them's the times when all of we should take care."

The same gipsy added that all crimes against women and children are committed in these periods of the moon, apparently when the power of Isis is at its lowest. It would be interesting to know what the statistics of Scotland Yard say on the subject. See also Crescent.

MOONSTONE

The birthstone of Cancer.

A very wonderful talisman, this beautiful stone with its milky brilliance and blue tint, symbolises the soft radiance of moonlight. In connection with the moonstone we get that familiar slang phrase, " Once in a blue moon " —meaning a very rare occurrence. According to Pavitt's " Book of Talismans," the Hindus say that the best variety of blue moonstones are washed up by the tides when the sun and moon are in very harmonious relation, at intervals of twenty-one years (three periods of the moon, whose number is seven) and from this has come the saying to express a lengthy period.

The moonstone is worn as a mascot to reconcile lovers who have parted, and medicinally as a cure for consumption, dropsy, or kidney troubles, besides which it protects travellers and brings general good fortune.

Also it was consulted as a guide for future conduct. If anyone is in doubt what to do, he should wait until the moon is waning, then place a moonstone in his mouth and fix his thoughts upon the business that is troubling him. Into his mind will come a determination to act in such and such a manner—and it is sure to be the right one !

MYRTLE

The flower sacred to Venus, and most fortunate to lovers. Until quite late years the myrtle was the English bridal flower, though recently it has been ousted by the orange blossom. It may be added that with British royal brides the myrtle is a favourite still.

NAILS

A rather unpleasant mascot is a nail drawn from a coffin or from a door leading into a vault. Such a nail hung above the bed banished all evil dreams.

NARITA

This word—the name of sacred shrine in Japan—is written on a thin piece of wood, and worn as a locket to protect against all ill. It is particularly powerful in bringing good fortune in business and to warding off dangers of travel.

NUMBERS

The following is a short account of the traditions clinging to our nine numbers. The foundation of these beliefs lie in the sacred faiths of long ago, and the table was compiled in forgotten ages, after deep research and thought.

ONE

This actually means The First, and as such was taken as the number of the First House of the Zodiac, Aries the Ram, which the Sun enters on March 21st, the beginning of our Spring, according to the modern calendars, the beginning of the year according to the ancient teaching which held Winter was the night when Nature slept, and Spring the dawn bringing new life to the world.

Aries is the First House of the astrological year and 1 —the Beginning—is its number.

All those who were born while the sun was in Aries will find 1 their fortunate number, which means that the 1st or 10th of any month will be fortunate dates on which they should begin new ventures.

One—the First—the Greatest—the Beginning—is a number given to the Sun, and though it belongs specially to Aries as the beginning of the year, it will be found fortunate also to those born under Leo, when the sun has its greatest power.

The number—or rather the influence for which it stands—has power to bestow plodding perseverance, courage and confidence on those who come under its influence, but in " ill aspected " cases these gifts may degenerate into stupid obstinacy.

TWO

Is one of the two numbers which have influence over the sign of Cancer, and those who come under its power will find the 2nd, 11th, or 20th of any month good.

Generally speaking, people to whom 2 is fortunate are possessed of a dual personality so that they are difficult to understand. Strictly honourable in most things as they may be, we find them lax in others, or they have the power of working extremely hard in some instances and then suddenly to fall under the curse of idleness for a time.

Often they have the Second Sight, or other psychic power, and many gifted seers and students of the occult have had 2 for their number—it is as if they had the power to glimpse each of two worlds.

The idea of the double influence is seen in many of the older myths and faiths. In the Heavens we find the Constellations of Gemini the Twins, and of Pisces the two fishes—on the staff of Mercury were two serpents—the Hindus say two bats are a sign of good wishes, and perhaps the same idea occurs in the old English rhyme concerning magpies, when we are told it is "One for sorrow, Two for mirth." A mascot in the shape of two fingers was common in Egypt, and Christian priests hold up two fingers as a sign of blessing. The Egyptians frequently wore two feathers in their headdresses, or little amulets made to represent two plumes, in which case the one stood for Honesty and the other for Knowledge.

THREE

Of all numbers this is the most sacred. In practically every religion of which we know it has a deep significance, and the ×, which is the Sign of the Unknown, is made up of triangles, a form of 3.

As a fortunate number it belongs to those born on the 3rd, 12th or 30th of any month, but its power is specially strong for those under the influence of Sagittarius or Pisces.

It is one of the Numbers of Jupiter, therefore it is very fortunate, and those to whom it belongs are capable of deeply religious feeling.

Of its sacred meaning in the Christian faith there is no need to write, but in almost every religion it has stood as the symbol of the Godhead. In ancient Egypt men worshipped the Trinity of the Father, the Mother and the Child—the Druids held that 3 was the Number of the

Unknown God, and venerated the three-leafed shamrock and mistletoe in His honour.   Wherever Buddhism is taught, men worship as Three in One—Buddha, his Word and his Church; while above all else they are taught they must attain the Three Virtues, which are Endurance, Courage and Obedience to the Law.

In folk-lore of all sorts 3 is most important.   Amongst the Romans a ring engraved with Three Ravens was worn to secure faithfulness in love—and the gipsies say three magpies in flight together is the certain sign that news of a wedding will be heard.   On the other hand, the same strange people declare that if three wild swans are seen flying together terrible misfortunes will follow. A woman in the New Forest told the writer, quite gravely, that not one of her people was surprised at the outbreak of war in 1914 because they had watched the wild swans all through the spring and summer and had noted how they flew in threes.

Another Romany belief is that if a dream comes three times it is certain to be true.

FOUR

Of all numbers this is considered the most fortunate, bestowing power and worldly success as well as the higher virtues. It is a number of Jupiter, the king of the gods, and tracing its traditions backwards we find it was sacred to Horus, the Rising Sun in ancient Egypt, to Baal, and to the Sun itself.

It belongs specially to those born under the sign of Leo, and it is good also to those born on the 4th, 13th, 22nd, or 31st of any month.   These people will find Sunday their fortunate day.   Amongst its other gifts it confers a generous and open-handed disposition, therefore those who come under its influence seldom remain rich. Though they attain wealth they give freely, never turning away from any appeal for help.

FIVE

The figure 5 is called the Soul Figure, or the Figure of Life, because it comes in the centre of the others, and may be said to represent the heart of all things.   In the same sense it was the symbol of the sun, the centre of the universe, thus it gives energy, activity, ambition, warmth and love—all that we mean when we speak of Life.

It was reverenced by the ancient Egyptians who credited it with special virtues because, apart from being the middle of all, it is made up of the first even and the first odd number, not counting 1. In Egypt and Greece the mere figure itself was held to be an important sigil or mascot, and as such was written on the walls of houses. And in many parts of England to-day there is the saying that a house which is Number Five is sure to be fortunate to its inmates—it would be interesting to know whether the doors of these fortunate houses have the figure large upon them.

From the earliest ages we can trace traditions of its powers and virtues in history, folk-lore, legend and myth. We are gifted with Five Senses; in Jewish history we read of five gifts given to the priests; of the five suits of clothes Joseph presented to his brethren, and how he presented only five of the latter to Pharaoh. David took five stones when he went to fight Goliath; Joshua hanged five kings on five trees, while—most important of all— every measurement of the Temple was either five or a multiple of five.

Astrology teaches that each planet has five aspects by which it rules. Mohemmedans hold to the Five Articles of Belief—our own Ten Commandments are a multiple of Five—in Freemasonry there are Five Points of Fellowship, and the mystic powers of the Five Pointed Star, the mascot of the Middle Ages, are dealt with under the head of " Star."

The Chinese have a mascot representing Five Bats, which stands for the Five Blessings—Long Life, Luck, Wealth, Health, and Peace.

As a birth number 5 belongs to those born under Gemini and Virgo, while it brings good fortune to those who were born on the 5th, 14th, or 23rd of any month.

Six

This is the number of Venus, so as a birth number belongs to those born under Taurus, also to Libra, and is fortunate to those born on the 6th, 15th or 24th of any month. As regards Libra people, astrology says every sixth year of their lives is marked by some event of importance.

When the influence of the number is all good, the greatest students and thinkers come under its power, but in cases where it is "ill aspected" it confers vulgar curiosity.

SEVEN

This is the number of those born under the sign of Cancer, and also belongs to those born on the 7th, 16th, or 25th of any month.

It is the number of lofty self-sacrifice and of all the higher virtues. Of its use in the most sacred part of the New Testament it would be improper to dwell here, but all is in keeping with the traditions of the number. The Old Testament tells us of the Seven Lamps of the Temple, in the New Testament there were the Seven Wise and the Seven Foolish Virgins, and in Egyptian lore the Ladder of Seven Steps was connected with most profound mysteries.

SEVEN GIFTS OF THE SPIRIT

In the Early Church it was taught that the Spirit confers Seven Gifts on the believer, the Gifts being—Wisdom, Understanding, Honour, Glory, Blessing, Strength and True Godliness.

Of the Seven Sleepers we have all heard, and country superstition declares that the seventh son of a seventh son has the power of healing, just as gipsies say the seventh daughter of a seventh daughter can tell the meanings of dreams. In common slang the term "Seven senses" is used.

SEVEN JEWELS

In Leadbeater's "Science of the Sacraments," he says the Altar should have Seven jewels embedded in it, to connect with the Seven Rays of Development under which Evolution takes place.

He gives these jewels, with their moral complements, as follows :—

1. Diamond (alternative crystal), for Strength.
2. Sapphire (alternative lapis laz., turquoise, sodalite), for Wisdom.
3. Emerald (alternative aquamarine, jade, malachite), for tact, adaptability.
4. Jasper (alternative chalcedony, agate, serpentine), for beauty.
5. Topaz (alternative citrine, stealite), for science, knowledge.
6. Ruby (alternative garnet, cornelian), for devotion.
7. Amethyst (alternative porphyry, violane), for ordered service (such as invokes Angelic help for a priest —hence the Bishop's ring also).

EIGHT

8 is a number of gloomy influence and almost unknown power. It is the emblem of Buddha and of Saturn and belongs to those born under Aquarius.

It is not considered a fortunate number, but as it belongs to Saturn, who is more favourable to old people than to children, thus it is probable that all who come under its influence will do well in middle and later life, though they may have many disappointments and troubles to face in youth.

NINE

9 is a mystic number which played its part in many ancient traditions and incantations, possibly because it is a multiple of Three. It belongs to those born under Scorpio, or on the 9th, 18th, or 27th of any month.

TO FIND YOUR LUCKY NUMBER

A very old astrological theory tells that in order to find the lucky number of any individual it is necessary to add together :—

The day of the month of birth.

The number of the month.

The number of the year.

The digit formed by the final adding is the luck bringer.

For example, we will suppose we want to find the number belonging to someone born July 7th, 1903, that is on the 7th of the seventh month.

$$\begin{array}{r} 7 \\ 7 \\ 1903 \\ \hline 1917 \end{array}$$

The casting is added again thus

$$\begin{array}{r} 1 \\ 9 \\ 1 \\ 7 \\ \hline 9 \end{array}$$

which brings the digit—the final result—as **9**. Hence 9 is the lucky number.

OLIVINE

The birth stone of Leo.

This and the peridot are both forms of the chrysolite, which see. When the colour of the stone verges on what we call olive green it is called the olivine, and as a charm should be set in gold—never in silver. It will give its wearer a happy outlook on life, make him fortunate in business and protect him from thieves.

ONYX

Really this is the sardonyx, which will be dealt with in due course, but the black variety is called by the shorter word. It is quite familiar as beads and necklaces, being black or very dark brown, with white marks upon it. Those born under Aries or Libra, or those who have Saturn antagonistic to them in any way should avoid the onyx. To them it will bring bad dreams at night and deep melancholy by day, besides involving them in quarrels and law suits. Yet it is a mascot to those who come under Saturn's influence in the right way, that is, people born under Capricorn or those whose birthday falls on the 8th, 17th, or 26th of any month (eight being the number of Saturn) or in a lesser degree to anyone born on a Saturday.

It is much used in beads for rosaries, as it has the power of inspiring deep devotion and holy thoughts.

OPALS

The idea that an opal is an unlucky stone is wrong according to astrology. It is specially fortunate to those whose birth-stone it is—that is, people born under Libra —though it only exercises its power for good on those who are unselfish and generous. Let a selfish person possess an opal, even though he be born under Libra and the stone a loving gift, and it will be useless as a charm if it is not actively antagonistic. In addition to Libra it is the birth-stone of those born under Taurus because of its association with Venus, whose power is always strong over Taurus folk.

It is the emblem of hope, perhaps because of its rainbow hues, and in the East is a sacred stone, typical of Truth. It gives foresight and the power of prophecy, but only if used for a good end. If the gifts conferred by an opal are misused certain misfortune will follow.

OTA-FU-KU

A Japanese talisman, the likeness of the goddess of good fortune. Generally she is represented by a laughing face painted on a purse or bag or other object that one friend may send to another. Even to look on her face will bring prosperity.

OWL

Is a greatly wronged bird, for its hooting is taken as a sign of misfortune or death. Yet the owl is the bird of Minerva, and is the symbol of wisdom. Mascots made in its likeness give success in anything requiring study.

PADLOCK

The presence of a padlock on any bunch of charms, but particularly if it is used to fasten a bracelet or bangle, is a symbol that the giver has secured the affections of the wearer and that the lock holds them safe. In addition the lock confers the blessings of long life and health and happiness.

In China there is a belief that the padlock must be made of silver in order to ensure the best results. There, if a father has an only son, or a son he loves very dearly, he will collect a hundred coins from the heads of a hundred different families, and from them make a silver padlock, with which he fastens a silver chain around the neck of his son.

PAGODA

A Chinese and Japanese mascot which gives inspiration and hope. Probably it is a form of the upright triangle. See Solomon's Seal.

PEACE (Mascots to Ensure)

The mascots which heal quarrels and bring together friends or lovers who have become estranged, are those which attract the influence of Mercury, the peace-making god, or rather Hermes, the older form of Mercury. Hermes was the inventor of musical instruments, he was the patron of harmony in every sense of the word, and did everything to elevate the thoughts, to inspire a love of the beautiful, to heal all discord in the world. For the peace-inspiring mascots see : Caduceus, Carbuncle, Dove, Harp, Laurel, Lyre, Moonstone, Olive Branch, and Turquoise.

PEARLS

That these beautiful gems represent tears is an old superstition which has been traced, more or less fancifully, to the fact that the pearl comes into being through suffering, even though the suffering be only that of an oyster, whose power of feeling we can hardly imagine very highly developed.

The pearl was dedicated to Isis, and was thought unfortunate to married people, though fashion decrees pearls are ideal ornaments for young girls, and many a bride defies superstition by wearing a rope of pearls with her wedding gown.

As mascots pearls are carried by Eastern divers as protection against sharks, and the Chinese swallow powdered pearls as a remedy for stomachic troubles. Amongst the Romans a mixture of powdered pearls and distilled water was a cure for lunacy.

Pearls are not attached to any of the heavenly bodies and therefore are not the birthstones of any date, but they are fortunate to all who have been born under a " Watery Sign."

PENNIES

There is a queer idea in many parts of England that good luck, in the way of unexpected windfalls or legacies, will come to those who keep a few pennies or other copper coins in the kitchen.

Probably the idea has arisen from the legends of fairies that haunt kitchens at night—often doing a good deal of useful work or at other times performing any amount of mischief. It was a widespread belief that in order to benefit by these weird little visitors offerings must be left where they could see them.

LEAP YEAR PENNIES

Pennies bearing the date of any Leap Year should be kept in the house. They will bring good fortune.

LEE PENNY

A very celebrated talisman of unknown origin is the Lee Penny, a silver coin—a groat of Edward I.—in which is set a heart-shaped red stone about half an inch long. The story goes that Sir Simon Locard of Lee set sail with Sir James Douglas, who carried the heart of Bruce in a golden casket that it might be buried in the Holy Land. Sir James was killed in Spain, but Sir Simon reached Palestine, where he did a great deal of fighting, and in one engagement took a powerful Emir prisoner, holding him to ransom.

The Emir's wife paid the sum demanded, apparently handing it to Sir Simon in person, for as she gave him the store of gold he noticed she dropped a small stone which did not seem of any worth, though she was frightened at her loss and insisted search should be made for it. Found it was, and then Sir Simon, seeing how much store she set by it, insisted it should be included in the ransom. She was most reluctant to part with it, but gave way in the end, and Sir Simon brought the red stone to Scotland, where it was mounted in the groat.

Before parting with the stone the lady explained its virtues to Sir Simon. Says Brand:—" It cured all diseases in cattle, and the bite of a mad dog in both man and beast. It is used by dipping the stone in water, which is given to the diseased cattle to drink; and the person who has been bit, and the wound or part infected is washed with the water.   There are no words used in the dipping of the stone, nor any money taken by the servants without incurring the owner's displeasure.   Many are the cures said to be performed by it. . . . When the plague was last at Newcastle the inhabitants sent for the Lee Penny and gave a bond for a large sum in trust for the loan; and they thought it did so much good they offered to pay the money and keep the Lee Penny, but the gentleman would not part with it.

"The most remarkable cure . . . was that of Lady Baird of Souchton Hall near Edinburgh, who having been bit by a mad dog was come the length of hydrophobia; upon which, having sent to beg the Lee Penny might be sent to her house, she used it for some weeks, drinking and bathing in the water it was dipped in and quite recovered.   This happened above eighty years ago, but is well attested, having been told by the lady of the then Laird of Lee, who died within these thirty years. . . . N.B.   It was tried by a lapidary and found to be a stone, but of what kind he could not tell."

PENTAGON

See Star.

PERIDOT

Is a golden green form of the Chrysolife, which has been dealt with both under its general name and also as the Olivine.   Except for its colour it is exactly the same as the latter and astrologically has the same attributes.

PHOENIX

The Chinese say likenesses of the mystic bird ensure long life and domestic happiness.   Mystically the phoenix represents the world : its head is the heavens, its eyes the sun, its beak the moon, its wings the wind, and its tail plants and trees.

Sir John Maundeville gives this account of the bird :— "In Egypt is the city of Heliopolis, that is to say, the city of the sun, in which there is a temple made round after the shape of the temple in Jerusalem.   The priests of that temple have all their writings dated by the bird called phoenix, of which there is but one in the world.

It comes to burn itself on the altar of the temple at the end of five hundred years, for so long it lives; and then the priests array their altar, and put thereon spices, and sulphur, and other things that will burn quickly, and the phoenix comes and burns itself to ashes. The next day they find in the ashes a worm, and the second day after they find a bird alive and perfect, and the third day it flys away. This bird is often seen flying in those countries; it is somewhat larger than an eagle, and has a crest of feathers on its neck greater than that of a peacock; its neck is yellow, its beak blue, its wings of a purple colour, and the tail is yellow and red. It is a handsome bird to look at against the sun, for it shines very gloriously and nobly."

PIGS

The belief that the pig is a luck bringer may have had a purely economical basis, as in the Irish saying which describes him as the gentleman who pays the rent. Yet the idea of the pig as a mascot is wide-spread. The Chinese make little pigs of gold or of silk to bring good fortune in trade, while in Ireland they tell you the figure of a pig is lucky only if it has had some part broken. Thus you buy mascots in the shape of pigs with one ear.

PILLOW

Charms in the form of cushions or pillows were Egyptian talismans, worn as preservation against sickness or any form of suffering.

PINE CONE

Most country boys will tell you that pine cones are bringers of good luck, and you will find cones in many cottages. In Greece and Rome the cones were emblems of the goddess Cybele, the acorn was sacred to her as well. She symbolised the fruitfulness of the earth, and was represented in a chariot drawn by lions with Atys, the youth she loved, by her side, carrying a pine tree.

In Rome her worship sank to a debased form, but she was worshipped as the mother, thus she was a form of Isis, and was the special deity of crops and harvests. It was the custom to fix pine cones on the tops of high posts in gardens and vineyards to implore her protection from blight, and often the cones would appear in the fronts of houses also. In Italy the custom remains, and in England the pine cone, carved in stone, is quite a common ornament on the pate-posts of gardens, or may be found in iron at the head of garden railings. Probably the good people to whom the gardens belong have little idea they are perpetuating the belief in a particularly earthbound goddess. See also Fir Tree.

PISCES
See Zodiac.

PLUMMET
A strangely shaped charm was the plummet, worn in ancient Egypt to attract Wisdom and Knowledge and Truth. It was the symbol of the god Thoth, inventor of all sciences, the reader of the secrets of all hearts.

POSY RINGS
See Rings.

RABBIT
Many modern mascots are in the likeness of more or less fascinating rabbits, and these seem particularly popular as luck bringers for motor cars. No ancient authority of their use can be found. Probably they belong to the same category as the Teddy Bear and the Golliwog.

RATS
The general belief in England is that rats are bringers of bad luck, that the sudden appearance of one in or near a house foretells trouble coming to those within. Probably the belief has no better foundation than the inborn dislike to vermin which most people know. In ancient Egypt the rat was a sacred animal, dedicated to Ra, the sun god, and both rats and mice were mascots and appear on many Egyptian monuments. See Mice.

RAVENS
As mascots, strengthen the memory, improve the health, and give strength to brain and body. Hugin (Thought) and Mumir (Memory) fly forth from Odin's palace, Hlidokialf daily to gather tidings of all that is happening in the world. That Noah despatched a raven from the Ark for the same purpose must not be overlooked.

RICE

When scattered at a wedding rice is intended as a mascot to bring good fortune to the bride and bridegroom, and its use comes from the East where rice is the symbol of fruitfulness and prosperity. In Saxon times wheat and barley were scattered in churches for brides to walk upon, so that the use of rice is not so much an innovation from the East, as an adaptation from the Saxons. See also Confetti.

RING

From the earliest ages the ring—symbol of Eternity—has been the token by which lovers plighted their troth. It is the bringer of all the good fortune, undying devotion, tender thoughts, and loving prayers can bestow.

Rings have been worn in all countries and at all times of which we have any knowledge, often as mere ornaments, but more generally as having some occult power or as representing some authority which the ring itself represented.

Thus Pharoah gave his ring to Joseph as a token he invested him with royal prerogatives—Judah's ring was a pledge of protection to his daughter-in-law in the future—and though the Bible tells us Boaz " plucked off his shoe and gave it to his neighbour and this is a testimony in Israel " modern authorities believe the word " shoe " is wrongly translated and that ring is intended.

According to Herodotus, the Babylonians wore rings on their fingers, and from them the custom spread to Greece, and then all over Europe. In Rome every freeman wore a ring of iron, and state officials wore rings as insignia of office. Somewhat similiar was the custom of the Anglo-Saxons, amongst whom all who were born of noble blood wore a torque—or ring—of gold round the throat.

BETROTHAL RINGS

Apparently it was not until the Middle Ages that the custom of a man giving a ring to the girl he has chosen as his future wife, became common. At that time the ceremony was called " handfastening," and when the ring was given it was understood the girl should go to her lover's house for a year and stay on trial, as it were, while he made up his mind whether he would marry her or not.

These " hand fast " rings were made of base metal in most cases, but often they were of plaited rush, so the term " rush ring weddings " came into use, meaning a very temporary contract indeed. Centuries later, when the handfast ceremony had become obsolete, silly girls used to believe there was something specially binding about a rush ring, and a good many seductions occurred in consequence.

Something resembling the " hand fast " lingers in Wales to the present day, and in Norway, at least in remote parts of the country, betrothals are considered almost as binding as actual marriages, and after the betrothal ceremony has taken place that of the wedding is often postponed for years.

In Iceland, until quite recently, it was the custom for the bridegroom to thrust his hand through a large ring when he took his bride's at the altar.

In the North of Scotland are many old stone monuments pierced with holes, and through the rings thus formed lovers in countless ages have clasped hands, believing that thus they made the keeping of their troth quite sure.

BYZANTINE RING

An amulet much worn in the Middle Ages as protection from the Evil Eye, and also against infection or from accident, was a ring bearing a shield engraved with a grotesque mask-like face from which radiated seven roughly shaped leaves to symbolise the Seven Gifts of the Spirit, *i.e.*, Power, Wisdom, Honour, Glory, Blessing, and Strength.

CRAMP RINGS

Silver rings engraved with the names of the Three Magi—Kaspar, Melchoir, and Balthasar—were worn during the Middle Ages as a charm against cramp.

GEMMEL RINGS

Apart from the " rush rings " or others used in the handfast ceremony, the gemmel ring was the forerunner of our engagement ring to-day and was used in the Middle Ages.

Each gemmel consisted of three rings, so made that they were held together by a clasp, the upper and lower rings being richly ornamented or jewelled, the middle one quite plain. At the betrothal the clasp was removed and the three rings taken apart over an open Bible. The first was placed on the hand of the bride elect, the other jewelled one on that of her future husband, while the third, the plainest of the three, was given to the witness who was present at the ceremony.

On the wedding day the three rings were joined by their clasp again, and placed on the hand of the bride—her wedding ring.

HALLOWED RINGS

Rings, especially if made out of the nails taken from old coffins or from the doors of church vaults, were very popular talismans in the Middle Ages, worn to cure cramp and kindred disorders. They were specially powerful if they had been blessed by the King or Queen—hence their name.

JASPER RINGS

Rings made of jasper or bloodstone were worn by the Egyptians to bring success in battle or in any undertaking which promised a hard struggle before success could be won. Later, signet rings set with bloodstones took the place of those old jasper rings and were worn for the same purpose.

MAGIC RINGS

Magic rings are mentioned in legends that are world-wide. We all know the Slave of the Ring who obeyed Aladdin, while the Koran credits Solomon with the possession of a magic ring which not only gave him power over all his enemies, but daily transported him to celestial spheres where he rested from the cares of state.

The Greeks had many stories of magic rings, most of which had the power of making their owners invisible, and in Greece and in Rome very large business must have been done in the sale of these and other rings which were acknowledged luck bringers.

MIZPAH RINGS

Of all token between lovers perhaps the mizpah ring is the most beautiful.

It may be an ordinary jewelled ring with the word " Mizpah " engraved within, but more usually it is of the signet pattern and has the word on a shield. In either case the reference is Biblical, and the word voices a prayer, meaning actually :—" The Lord watch between thee and me when we are absent one from another."

Thus the mizpah ring is particularly suitable as a gift between lovers who are likely to be parted for a while.

POSY RING

In the sixteenth and seventeenth centuries "posy rings " became the fashion—that is, rings within which a line or two of rhyme was engraved. Very curious some of these efforts at poetry were, voicing many different ideas. For instance :—

> Our contract
> Was Heaven's act

is quite a charming sentiment for a bridegroom to express, as is also :—

> In thee, my choice,
> Do I rejoyce.

But a note of doubt seems to have crept into :—

> God above,
> Increase our love.

A very old couplet, hardly yet out of date, had its origin in these posy rings :—

> When this you see
> Remember me.

Sometimes the writers of these verses introduced a touch of comedy that was not always in the best possible taste, as in the case of the Right Reverend Dr. John Thomas, Bishop of Lincoln, who ought to have known better. He had buried three wives, and when he became engaged to the lady who was to be his fourth, he gave her a ring on which he had inscribed :—

> If I survive
> I'll make them five.

One wonders what were the thoughts of the lady when that ring was placed on her hand.

When the outside of the ring had the design of clasped hands upon it, the usual " posy " ran :—

> Not two but one
> Till life is gone.

In the same way, when a heart appeared outside a ring, the inside motto was :—

> My heart and I,
> Until I die.

SALUS RINGS

In Rome, special rings dedicated to the goddess Salus—who was also Hygeia—were worn as protection against all disease or infection, and to ensure general good fortune. They were engraved with a five-pointed star (see Star) surrounded by mystic letters and a coiled serpent —the symbol of healing.

SIGNET RINGS

In the days when writing was a rare accomplishment the signet ring was of grave importance—impressed upon molten wax it gave the authority of its wearer to any written bond or message, and if the ring itself was sent it became the token of authority passed from one hand to another. Naturally care was taken in the choice of the stones on which the all important signet was engraved, and those stones were in astrological keeping with the birthdate of the wearer.

VICTORIAN ENGAGEMENT RINGS

In the early nineteenth century the engagement ring as we know it became popular. The most fashionable of those early ones were set with stones that were not chosen for their harmony of colouring nor for their intrinsic beauty, but because their initial letters formed some appropriate word, thus :—

Ruby, Emerald, Garnet, Amethyst, Ruby, Diamond—**REGARD**.

Lapis-Lazuli, Opal, Verde-Antique, Emerald, Malachite, Emerald—**LOVE ME**.

Snake Rings

A ring in the form of a coiled snake has the power of endowing its wearer with long life and good health, but when two snakes are coiled to form a ring, their heads facing each other, that ring acts as peacemaker between friends who have quarrelled.

Talismanic Rings

When Edward the Confessor visited Jerusalem, he brought back a ring which was long preserved in Westminster Abbey as a talisman that effected cures in cases of cramp and epilepsy when touched by those afflicted. So far its fame spread it became one of the most celebrated of talismanic rings. But there were many others. In the sixteenth century a very popular talisman was a ring with the Hebrew word MUSSELTAUB inscribed upon it. Evidently it was of Jewish origin, the word meaning, "We wish you good fortune."

CLADDAGH RING

Wedding Rings

The wedding ring plays a part in all sorts of charms—a wart rubbed nine times with a wedding ring will disappear, and a girl who wants to dream of her future husband or to see his wraith, can work all sorts of charms by aid of a borrowed wedding ring.

In Chambers' "Book of Days" he tells of a community of fisher-folk living in the Claddagh, Galway, who seldom inter-marry with their neighbours. Thus they cling to many old customs, and one of these is the use of curious wedding rings which bear the device of two clasped hands holding a heart. These rings are heirlooms, passing from the mother to her eldest daughter—apparently the mother ceasing to wear a ring when her daughter marries—and so going from one generation to another.

The custom remotely suggests the Cumberland one, of

invariably bestowing the mother's Christian name upon the eldest daughter. Many Border families can show how a Christian name has been used in an unbroken line for centuries.

The Jews, who retain so many old customs, place the greatest importance on the ring at both the betrothal and marriage ceremonies. They insist that at marriage it has to be of a certain value and the actual property of the bridegroom, bought by him, not given nor lent. From the moment he puts the ring on the bride's finger, calling all present to witness that henceforward she is consecrated to him, she becomes his wife according to Jewish law.

Probably from the Jewish insistence that the ring must be of a certain worth comes the very common superstition to be found all over England, that a marriage is not legal unless the ring used is of pure gold, the only substitute allowed being the ring in the handle of the key of the church door.

This is absurd. In our Registry Office ceremony the ring plays no part, and in the Church service a ring of any value may be used. When the proper ring has gone amissing from some cause or another, one can generally be borrowed from a spectator, but failing that the handle of the key has been resorted to in extreme cases.

ZODIACAL RINGS

Very ancient rings were inscribed with the signs of the Zodiac, and in these cases the circle of the ring itself was symbolical of the pathway of the sun round the heavens.

LEGENDS OF RINGS

Very quaint are the theories old writers brought forward to account for the popularity of rings. In the seventeenth and eighteenth centuries particularly there was a rage for explaining everything, and during the Commonwealth, when it was realised that the ring had certainly come to us from the heathens, there was an agitation on foot to make the wearing of all rings—even wedding rings—illegal.

It was about that time there was published a book entitled " A Treatise on Spousals," in which the writer tells us of the invention of the ring thus :—

"The first inventor of the ring as reported was one Prometheus. The workman which made it was Tubal Cain, and Tubal Cain, by the counsel of our first parent, Adam (as my author telleth me) gave it to his son to this end that therewith he should espouse a wife, like as Abraham delivered unto his servants bracelets and rings of gold. The form of a ring being circular and without end, importeth this much, that their mutual love and hearty affection should roundly flow from one to the other as in a circle, and that continuously and forever."

In this connection it is interesting to find that the name Tubal Cain has been traced to the Persian "tupal," meaning bronze, and "kayn" the Arabic for smith. Of course the Bible gives us Tubal Cain as the brother of Jabal and Jubal, and the traditional ancestor of all workers in metal.

ROBIN

Wherever a robin appears he is a bringer of good luck so long as he is not injured nor driven away, and the person who happens to see a robin flying high in March may be sure of good health the rest of the year.

To find a robin's nest with eggs in it is particularly fortunate, but great care must be taken not to disturb the nest, while dire consequences will follow those who dare to take a robin's egg.

ROD OF MERCURY

See Caduceus.

ROMANY MASCOTS AND BELIEFS

See Acorn, Agate, Bee, Blackthorn, Broomstick, Daisy, Doorstep, Dove, Elder, Foxglove, Hare, Key, Marsh Mallow, Moon, Numbers, Serpent, Twisted Root, and Wagtail.

ROSEMARY

A sprig of rosemary is a pretty mascot for lovers or for friends who are parted by distance to send to each other. Rosemary means remembrance, and the sprig has power to keep the sender in the loved one's thoughts. Astrologically it is a herb of Aries, therefore is particularly powerful for those born under that sign. In the

Language of Flowers it signifies remembrance, and as that language came to us from the East we may take it that the belief in this particular attribute is world-wide.

Nor was its power occult only; it seems to have been physical as well. Old physicians prescribed a decoction of rosemary drunk early in the morning for strengthening the memory, while astrologers taught that a rosemary leaf carried in the pocket would prevent forgetfulness.

From the most ancient days rosemary played its part at both weddings and funerals. It was found in the bride's bouquet and on the coffin—always with the idea of symbolising enduring love and a tie that would never be forgotten.

Apparently the wood of the rosemary bush was used for many purposes, for in a work entitled " Eachard's Observations," published in 1672, we find :—

" I cannot forget him, who having at some time or the other been suddenly cured of a little headache with a rosemary posset, would scarce drink out of anything but rosemary cans, cut his meat with a rosemary knife, and pick his teeth with a rosemary sprig."

RUBY

As a birth-stone belongs to Capricorn, to whose people it will bring health and happy love. It reconciles those who have quarrelled, and guards its wearer against dangers of storm or flood.

The true ruby is one of the most beautiful of jewels and its colour is always red, though it may vary from pink to deepest crimson. A stone called the spinel was confused with the true ruby until recent times, and spinels —though generally red—have been found orange, green, violet, and blue in colour. Both the ruby and the spinel are the same astrologically. The ancients absolutely identified them, though modern geologists class them in different categories.

In the East the ruby has ever been a most popular talisman. It is worn to ward off attacks of enemies, and to give warning of danger from poison, or of coming trouble, by changing its colour.

RUE

A sprig of rue, or a little bag containing the dried leaves of rue, was a powerful charm against witchcraft in the Middle Ages.   Therefore rue was an important luck bringer.

S.

In many places you will see pieces of iron shaped as the letter S fastened to the outside walls of old houses, and it is often said they have been placed against the brickwork as a support. This is wrong. They are mascots to secure the house against destruction by fire. Generally one S is used, but sometimes there are two, and occasionally the S has a bar across the middle. Another form of the same mascots is two crescents placed back to back. In every case the meaning is the same.

SA

The " sa " was an Egyptian mascot made in metal rather in the form of a man's cravat, the actual meaning of the word being " tie." It was worn to secure protection from all ills, and was the symbol of the hippopotamus-headed goddess Ta-urt, who personified Divine wisdom and human reason.

SAILORS (Special Mascots for)

See Aquamarine, Anchor, Caul, Emerald, Shell.

SAGITTARIUS

See Zodiac.

SALT

The ancients, seeing salt was incorruptible, called it the emblem of Immortality. Its name was given from Salus the Roman goddess of Health, whom the Greeks called Hygeia, and as many days in the year were set apart as festivals in her honour and salt took an important part in the ceremonies, it is easy to see how traditions gathered round it.

The fact that salt foretold the coming of wet weather by growing damp—as most people know from the seaweed which makes the best of all weather-glasses—was early recognised. In an old book called " Nature's Secrets," the author, Willsford, writes :—

" Salt extracted out of the earth, water, or any mineral, hath these properties to foreshew the weather : for if well kept in fair weather it will be dry and apt to dissolve against wet into its proper element; on boards it hath lain upon and got into the pores of the wood, it will be dry in fair and serene weather, but when the air inclines to wet it will dissolve; and you shall see the board venting his brackish tears; the salt-cellars will have a dew upon them, and those made of metal look dim against rainy weather."

In honour of the goddess, Salus, nurses put a pinch of salt into the mouths of newly-born infants—to-day they use borax, which is a salt, as a safeguard against the thrush—and when a cow had calved, a pinch of salt had to be added to the first pail of milk which was taken from her.

Both Greeks and Romans made a special point of mixing salt with their sacrificial cakes, and salt was flung on altar fires. When anything so sacred as salt was allowed to fall to the ground, the carelessness would arouse the wrath of Salus, and so bring ill fortune, hence to spill salt is said to be unlucky. Probably also this has reference to the belief that no mascot should be allowed to touch the ground.

The importance of salt was maintained long after the worship of Salus had been forgotten. Almost till modern times—certainly throughout the Middle Ages—the table of the nobleman was divided across the middle by a giant salt-cellar. Those who sat above it were the chief and his guests, while humbler people sat below.

" He's not worth his salt " is a common saying that goes back to classic times, meaning he does not deserve the protection of Salus.

In Scotland and Ireland it was the custom to lay a plate containing a pinch of earth and one of salt on the breast of the newly dead, the earth representing the body which was corruptible, and the salt standing for the immortal spirit.

See Salus Ring.

SAPPHIRE

The birth-stone of Taurus and Capricorn.

Around this stone a thousand beautiful legends cling, and there is a world-wide belief that it will only keep its deep, rich colouring if worn by one who is true to love. The Buddhists say it produces the spirit of devotion and of earnest prayer, that it elevates the thoughts and will confer happiness so long as its wearer leads a pure and honest life.

The Jews saw in it a sacred stone, and in the Bible we are told that the ring of Solomon contained a sapphire. In the twelfth century Pope Innocent III. ordered that the rings of the bishops should be of pure gold, set with sapphires.

It shared with the emerald the power of preserving the sight, especially in cases of smallpox, where if the eyes were rubbed with a sapphire it was said no harm would come to the sight. In old St. Paul's there was a celebrated sapphire presented by " Richard de Preston, Citizen and Grocer," which was kept in the church that all who suffered from any affliction of the sight might apply the stone to the eyes. We are not told of any attempts made to sterilise it after each application.

STAR SAPPHIRES

Occasionally cloudy stones, called " star sapphires," are found, their name being given from the fact that owing to some peculiarity in their construction, six rays of light invariably emanate from them. Anciently they were the Astrea—the Star Stones—and were specially powerful mascots for lovers.

SARDONYX

The birth stone of Aquarius.

The true sardonyx is a red-brown stone with a layer of white passing through it—when the white is absent the stone is the cornelian. It has been dealt with under the heading " Oynx," but in its red-brown form is particularly powerful against the bites of snakes and all venomous creatures, while if hung round the neck will bring relief from pain, whatever the cause.

SCALES

In ancient Egypt the scales were used in connection with the worship of Isis, probably in the same connection as the Romans afterwards showed scales held in the hand of their blindfolded figure of Justice. As mascots, scales are particularly powerful to those who have suffered unjustly for any cause, also they influence the thoughts to see both sides of a question, and to weigh the pros and cons of any case.

Scales are the symbol of the Zodiacal House of Libra the Balance. See Zodiac.

SCARAB

See Beetle.

SCORPION

See Zodiac.

SEA HORSE

See Horse.

SERPENTS

Since the dawn of history man has seen the symbol of all that is wonderful in the serpent. From its extreme length of life the creature was held to typify wisdom and old age, while when shown with its tail in its mouth it became a ring, the emblem of Eternity.

When the serpent became first typical of evil is doubtful, so far back is the legend lost in the mists of antiquity. We are all familiar with the story of his tempting Eve in the Garden of Eden, while in ancient Egypt, though the serpent was worn on the brow of Pharaoh as an imperial crown and was honoured for his wisdom, he was hated as the disguise of Typhon, the murderer of Osiris the god, yet he was worshipped as the god of the Setting Sun, in contrast to Horus, god of the Rising Sun.

Some remains of the tradition which claimed the serpent as the god of the Setting Sun linger in our own land. In many a village you will be told that no matter what you do to a snake it will never die until the sun is setting.

Though the Egyptians feared a serpent as a possible form of Typhon, they respected his learning, and because he was the symbol of Eternity they painted his likeness at the door of every tomb. They watched him change

his skin, and, throwing off the shabby covering, emerge
glittering into the light. Here, they said, was a sign of
Immortality, and as such he must be reverenced.

THE SNAKE'S HEAD

Has always been considered a particularly fortunate
mascot, and the Romans believed that the likeness of a
serpent in the house would secure its inmates against
plague and other sickness.

SNAKES' SKINS

Gipsies never pass the cast skin of a snake if they see
it on the roadside. The skin of an adder seems to be
regarded as a charm, but the skin of a harmless snake is
treasured, and a piece of it laid on boil or sore or wound
is said to work a certain cure—another of the many links
by which tradition connects the serpent with the art of
healing. See Ring.

SHAMROCK

Trefoil of all kinds has been given a religious significance through the countless ages during which the
doctrine of a Trinity has been believed.

The present belief in the luck of the shamrock and in
the magic powers possessed by one that has four leaves,
are generally traced to the Druids.

These ancient priests and law-givers taught the
existence of One God alone—mystic—mighty—unseen.
Probably that was a Druid altar which St. Paul found in
Athens dedicated to " The Unknown God."

They held that three was the sacred number, and thus
the clover and the shamrock were sacred symbols to
them.

The Druids passed. Savage races blotted out that un-
written learning which had swayed the world for
centuries—then Christianity arose and spread the more
rapidly because the people were filled with faint traditions
of that old, old faith which had worshipped One God, and
yet had reverenced the Three.

England was practically Christianized when Saint
Patrick crossed to Ireland on his missionary journey, and
when he landed, the Irish, led by Druids, combated his
teaching. In particular the people could not understand

the mystery of the "Three in One," till Saint Patrick gathered a shamrock and held it up as proof of what he taught. Another version goes that the shamrock was unknown in Ireland until Saint Patrick introduced it as an object lesson. That story is not to be found in any of the early lives of Saint Patrick, and there would have been no need for him to introduce the plant as any other trefoil would have done as well.

More probably the shamrock was revered as a mystic emblem in Ireland long before Saint Patrick, but the Saint was quick to take advantage of the fact, and afterwards it became adopted as Ireland's national emblem.

The shamrock—the green immortal shamrock,
Chosen leaf of bard and chief,
Old Erin's native shamrock.

The elder Pliny writes of the shamrock, declaring it is a sacred and magic plant since no serpent will touch it, and here we may get another link with Saint Patrick— it is said he introduced the shamrock to Ireland and that he banished all snakes from the country. At first sight there is no connection between the legends, but on second thoughts—one wonders.

At any rate the shamrock became venerated in Ireland, and because it was watched and loved for its associations it was a frequent gift between lovers and friends, and so was a mascot.

Then it was noticed that while four leafed clovers are fairly common, the Lesser Yellow Trefoil—as botanists call the shamrock—is very rarely found with more than three leaves. It became a common saying that a shamrock, being a symbol of all that is holy, of patriotism and lofty thoughts, must bring a blessing to those who wear it, but if one with four leaves could be found it would bestow upon its discoverer the power of gratifying every wish. Of course it was a superstition—a joke, if you care to put it so—but the saying became widespread and has had many believers.

SHEEP

In many parts of the country there is a saying that to meet a flock of sheep at the moment a wish has formed in your mind is a sign that the wish will be granted. In the Midlands they tell you that when seeing the first lamb of the spring it is important to notice the point of view from which the little animal appears. If his tail is towards you the year will be unlucky, if he is facing you expect good fortune.

SHELL

In many ways, by many creeds, shells have been sacred emblems.

THE CONCH SHELL

Is one of the Eight Glorious Emblems of Buddha, while from the fact that when a shell is held to the ear a murmur is heard, arose the poetic fancy that the sound of the waves forever haunts its depths.

There came the idea that a shell has power to guard those far from home, forming a link between the traveller and those he had left behind. Nearly all who have a sailorman in the family possess conch shells brought from Indian seas. To-day they are used as ornaments or stored in museums; that they were once called mascots has been forgotten.

THE SCALLOP SHELL

Is an emblem of Saint James the Great, and his shrine at Compostella, in Galicia, is ornamented with shells—from which all pilgrims who visited the shrine were permitted to carry scallop shells in their hats, just as good Moslems wear the green turban after a pilgrimage to Mecca.

But why were these shells used to decorate the apostle's grave?

One theory suggests that as the shores around Compostella abound with these fish, their shells were used to mark the resting place of the saint until his tomb could be prepared. But surely that is puerile.

Spanish legend states that Saint James visited Spain and taught Christianity to the people of Galicia, so when he left them to return to Jerusalem his thoughts and interests remained with his converts. In Jerusalem, martyrdom at the hands of Herod Agrippa was his fate, but, for some reason unexplained, his body was placed in a little boat with sails set, and the winds carried it straight back to the coast of Spain—to the scene of his missionary labours. A beautiful story this, read in the right light, and with it in the mind it is easy to conclude that the shells on the shrine are not shells at all, but are copies of some rude attempt to represent the sail which guided the barque across the sea.

Yet another legend may be told concerning this Saint James, since it concerns his shrine though has no mention of the shell.

According to an MS. in the Bodleian Library, long, long before the Christian era, a daughter of Pharaoh, who was named Scota, fell under the influence of Moses and learnt to worship the God of the Israelites. She was loved by Gathelus, son of Cecrops, who laid the foundations of Athens, and in order to escape the plagues of Egypt, she and her lover fled to Spain, carrying with them a sacred relic she seems to have stolen from the Israelites—unless she obtained permission to take it away.

This relic was the large square stone which had formed the pillow at Bethel on which Jacob had slept, when he dreamed his dream, and which he afterwards dedicated as an altar.

Gathelus and Scota landed at Compostella : there they founded a town and built their temples. When we remember that in the Latin the names of Jacob and James are both represented by Jacobus the association takes an added interest. The mention of Bethel is believed to be a later addition, but in this legend also we get the idea of a ship coming from the East, bearing something infinitely holy, something connected with the name of Jacobus, and carrying it to Compostella.

The legend goes on that Gathelus " sate as king upon his marble chair in Brigantia," and that his son, Hyberus, took the sacred stone with him when he led an argosy to colonise the island which became Ireland—or Hibernia in his honour—while its new inhabitants were called the Scots in memory of his mother.

For ages the stone remained at Tara as a coronation throne, then Fergus carried it to Iona, where added

sanctity was given it because Columba, the Saint—
evidently believing the story of its association with Bethel
—laid his head upon it as he was dying.

That association with Columba we may take as historic,
and the rest of its story is clear. King Kenneth carried
the stone to Scone, in A.D. 850, that it might serve as a
coronation throne, and there it remained until A.D. 1296
when Edward Longshanks heard the legend that whoso
owns the stone will rule many lands. He brought it to
Westminster, dedicated it to the Confessor, and set it
beside the altar in the Abbey.

In the Abbey it remains. With the exception of Queen
Mary Tudor every English sovereign has been crowned
on it since it was brought South. At one period it seems
to have been magnificently carved and gilded; it was a
throne indeed, though at recent coronations it has been
hidden under cloth of gold during the ceremony. But
whether hidden or not, the stone remains a sacred relic,
and even allowing for much legend, its history can be
traced far back through the ages.

To return to Saint James the Great and his scallop
shell :—

The idea that the shell is a mascot ensuring the safety
of travellers can be traced to those voyages from the
East which concerned Compostella, and from there also
came the idea that whoever should give help to the owner
of the shell—*i.e.,* to one who had made a pilgrimage to
the shrine—would surely win blessings in return.

Grotto Day

That tradition of St. James and the Scallop Shell is
remembered in London in a rather strange way. Every
year on July 25 (the date of the Saint's martyrdom) small
boys run after passers-by in the streets, and holding out
oyster shells—it is seldom scallop shells are seen—utter
the entreaty :—

" Please remember the grotto."

Some few go further, and in quiet corners build up
little grottos of shells or lay out ornaments of grass and
flowers. Indeed the writer has seen picture postcards
and cigarette cards arranged in a pattern on the pavement

by an urchin who sat back on his heels to admire his " grotto."

Until a few years ago " Grotto Day " was a regular institution of the London streets. Quite elaborate grottos were built, often with lighted candles inside, and the youngsters must have reaped quite a good harvest as the reward of their industry.

And every grotto was a memorial to Saint James, Apostle and Martyr, and a reminder of his shrine, though few of the children, or of the people who flung them coppers, had any idea that it was so.

SHINENAKA

A Japanese mascot, which is hung across doorways and before houses at the New Year to prevent evil spirits entering the house. The shinenaka was a rope from which were suspended bunches of rice straw that had been plucked up by the roots—straw thus gathered having special power.

SHIP

SHIP

As a mascot this has a religious signification. It was adopted by the early Christians to represent the Church, and rings or brooches or household ornaments made in its likeness helped their owners to resist temptations of the world, the flesh, and the devil, besides forming a silent confession of faith. The illustration is of a Greek mascot, the actual ship shown being the sign of the Island of Corfu.

SHOES

The traditions concerning shoes are very old and very numerous. Probably everyone has heard that an old shoe is a lucky gift, hence we throw old shoes after the bride and bridegroom when they start on their honeymoon, while gipsies say that if a girl has lost her lover he will come back if she will put her shoes outside the window of her bedroom at night. Also that a girl will have good luck in her love affairs and happy dreams if she places her shoes beside her bed with the heel of the one to the middle of the other. Evidently this is a form of the Tau Cross.

SIGIL

Correctly a sigil is a signature or sign used to denote some occult or magical word. Sigils as charms were carried on the person, usually in little bags or lockets hung round the neck, or they were engraved on rings or other articles of jewellery or on the sword blades of soldiers, always in the belief that they would protect their owner from dangers of every kind whether besetting the soul or the body.

SACRED DIAGRAM *

Perhaps the most frequent of all sigils—as it was reputed to be the most powerful—was the mystic word Abracadabra, which see.

Other important sigils are :—

AGLA

This word which is formed of the initial letters of the Latin words in the sentence " Thou are mighty forever, O Lord," was inscribed on the inside of many rings during the Middle Ages.

ANANIZAPTA

Another sigil engraved within rings in the fourteenth and fifteenth centuries. It was worn to protect its wearer from epilepsy or drunkenness and was particularly powerful if worn at the same time as a Tau Cross.

* Reprinted by kind permission of William Rider & Son, Ltd., from the " Book of Talismans," by W. T. and K. Pavitt.

CRUTCH

See under separate head.

DIAGRAM

The Lucky Diagram is a Hindu mascot, one of the Eight Glorious Emblems of Buddha.

ENGRAVED RING

See Ring.

FIGURE FIVE

See Numbers.

JOCHEBED

See under separate head.

MONOGRAMME

The sacred Monogramme of Thoth, god of Wisdom, was in the shape of a Tau Cross standing on a circle. It was a very powerful sigil, particularly guarding against hidden dangers, since it symbolised the god of Wisdom presiding over the world and eternally protecting it.

NARITA

See under separate head.

SIMSUM

This word was an astrological talisman in whose powers the belief was very wide-spread, its letters containing the initials of the planets in their correct order thus :—Saturn, Jupiter, Mars, Sun, Venus, Mercury— the letters " J " and " I," and " V " and " U " being, of course, identical in the older alphabets.

SEVEN ANGELS

The names of the Seven Angels written in red formed a very powerful sigil. See Angels.

TABLE OF JUPITER

See Table.

THE THREE MAGI

The names of the three magi, which are given traditionally as Caspar (white), Melchoir (light), and Baltasar (Lord of the Treasure House) were a sigil. In this connection there is a very old legend which professes to tell how to find anything that is lost.

To work the charm, get a piece of wax, melt it in the oven and pour it on a plate so that it sets smooth and firm. On it, with a nail or pin or any sharp instrument, write the names of the Three Magi. Put the wax under your pillow and you will dream of the whereabouts of whatever you have lost. It was not only missing articles which were traced this way, but absent lovers, relations, and friends as well.

SILVER

Belongs to four of the Houses of the Zodiac—Gemini, Cancer, Virgo, and Pisces.

As gold was dedicated to Osiris—the Sun—so silver was sacred to Isis, and in ancient times was hardly secondary in value to gold. Because of its beauty and purity and association with the goddess, it plays its part in many spells and charms. In China the father who has an only son collects a hundred silver coins from as many different families, and these are formed into a padlock (which see). In many respects this reminds one of the old English remedy for fits. The parents of the child so afflicted stand in the church porch on Sunday mornings and collect thirty silver sixpences from thirty unmarried men who have attended the service. These sixpences are carried by a bachelor to a smith or worker in metals, who must be a bachelor also, and by him are made into a necklace. It was believed that by wearing that necklace constantly the sufferer would be cured.

The Bible contains many mentions of silver, always with reference to its extreme value and beauty. In the Vision of Nebuchadnezzar the mighty figure which appeared to the king had " breast and arms of silver," and concerning this Dr. Hales says :—" The arms and shields of the Persians were frequently ornamented with silver : whence Alexander instituted that remarkable body of veteran infantry, called Argyraspides from their silver shields, after the conquest of Persia, adopting the manners of the conquered nation."

In the twelfth Psalm the singer says the words of the Lord are " pure as tried silver "—as being the rarest and most faultless of earthly things.

SOLDIERS (Special Mascots for)

See Beetle, Bells, Bloodstone, Carbuncle, Silver, Wheel Cross.

SOLOMON'S SEAL

Few mystic signs are more familiar than this that has been adopted by the Freemasons—we all know the two triangles which adorn so many watch chains and appear on masonic buildings.

It is a beautiful, soul-strengthening sign, and is a powerful mascot, preserving its wearer from the perils of travel and from occult evil.

Tradition says it was the Seal of Solomon, and as such was carved upon his temple at Jerusalem. Quite probably he did place it there, as the Symbol of Ancient Wisdom, for it is much, much older than his time. It has been connected with almost every religion or faith of which we have trace, and always the triangle with its point upwards has stood for Love, Truth, and Wisdom.

With the Egyptians it had this meaning, but stood for their Trinity as well. The Druids saw in it the emblem of the Mystic Three, while in old India it stood for Brahma, the Creator; Vishnu, the Preserver; and Siva, the Destroyer.

So much for the upright triangle. The other represents the material world as opposed to the Spiritual. While the one stands for Love, Truth, and Wisdom, the other represents the World, the Flesh, and the Devil. The two intertwined show the eternal lesson that Good—pointing upwards—must triumph over the Evil, that is being forced into the depths.

See also under Star.

SOUTHERNWOOD

Astrology says Southernwood is a herb of Mercury, but it is the special plant for lovers, nevertheless, and lovers' vows uttered near a bush of Southernwood will be surely kept. As a mascot a sprig should be gathered and put away in any gift which the lover has made.

All over England Southernwood is called by one of two names—either Old Man or Lad's Love, and, as "old man" is a frequent term for a husband, we may conclude that both names have somewhat the same meaning. The charm in which it plays a part is well known. If a girl wishes to discover whether she is loved or no, she gathers a sprig of Southernwood, speaking her lover's name at the same time. Laying the sprig on the palm of one hand, she claps the two together so that the sprig is bruised. If afterwards it gives out a faint odour her lover is wavering or false, but if the scent is strong so will be his devotion.

SPEAR

Always a symbol of power. In Norse mythology Odin's spear, which he named Gungner, gave him victory in battle, and in Japan the god Bishamon is portrayed holding the Spear of Glory.

SPIDER

The belief that the spider has power to bring good or evil fortune is very ancient. It was popular with the Romans, who had a favourite mascot in the shape of a precious stone on which a spider was engraved. Also they were fond of carrying little spiders of gold or silver or any of the fortunate metals, to bring success in anything to do with trade.

The spider we call the Money Spinner is the living representative of these Roman mascots.

The idea that to kill a spider will bring bad luck is common still, and most housewives, while destroying the web, will carefully lift the spider and put it out of doors. That killing a spider is followed by a monetary loss is the belief in some parts of the country, thus particularising the kind of ill luck to be expected. But to see a spider is fortunate so long as it is not hurt.

The French vary the legend slightly. According to them the sight of a spider in the house is not fortunate in the forenoon, but if you see it in the afternoon you may certainly expect a present, the value of the gift increasing according to the lateness of the hour. They agree that in neither case must the creature be hurt.

BRUCE AND THE SPIDER

Always the spider has been taken as the symbol of thrift and industry—for very obvious reasons—and there is the well-known story how Robert the Bruce, worn out by ill fortune, almost gave up his struggle for the crown until encouraged by a spider.

In " Tales of a Grandfather " the story is told **thus** :—

" The news of the taking of Kildrummie, the capture of his wife, and the execution of his brother, reached Bruce while he was residing in a miserable dwelling at Rachrin, and reduced him to the point of despair.

" It was about this time that an incident took place which, although it rests only on tradition . . . is rendered probable by the manners of the time. . . . Bruce was lying one morning on his wretched bed and deliberating with himself whether he had not better resign all thoughts of attempting to make good his right to the Scottish crown. . . . While he was doubtful of what he should do, Bruce was looking upward to the roof of the cabin in which he lay; and his eye was attracted by a spider, which, hanging at the end of a long thread of its own spinning, was endeavouring, as is the fashion of that creature, to swing itself from one beam in the roof to another, for the purpose of fixing the line on which it meant to stretch its web.

" The insect (sic.) made the attempt again and again without success; and at length Bruce counted that it had tried to carry its point six times, and had been as often unable to do so. It came into his head that he himself had fought just six battles against the English and their allies, and that the poor, persevering spider was in exactly the same situation with himself, having made as many trials, and been as often disappointed in what it aimed at.

" ' Now,' thought Bruce, ' as I have no means of knowing what is best to be done, I will be guided by the luck that shall attend this spider. If the insect shall make another effort to fix its thread, and shall be successful, I will venture a seventh time to try my fortune in Scotland; but if the spider shall fail I will go to the wars in Palestine and never return to my native country more.'

" While Bruce was forming this resolution, the spider made another effort with all the force it could muster, and fairly succeeded in fastening its web to the beam which it had so often in vain attempted to reach. Bruce, seeing the success of the spider, resolved to try his own fortune; and as he had never before gained a victory, so he never afterwards sustained any considerable or decisive defeat. I have often met people of the name of Bruce so completely persuaded of the truth of this story, that they would not on any account kill a spider; because it was that insect which had shown the example of perseverance, and given the signal of good luck to their great namesake."

SPINEL

See Ruby.

STAG

See Deer.

STAR

Considering that practically all the earliest religions were founded on the study of the heavens, it is little wonder star-shaped talismans have been credited with special powers as being closely connected with the wonders of the Infinite they represent.

Any jewel or pendant in the shape of a star is fortunate, and stars appear in church architecture, on royal robes, on insignias of State, always as emblems of good, as mascots which fight evil.

FIVE POINTED STARS

Of all star talismans that which is called the pentagon or pentacle, the five pointed star is the most important, since by its aid the powers of evil might be bound so that they were rendered helpless against mankind. Solomon's Seal was given the same attribute, as in the Arabian Nights' story of the fisherman who found " a bottle of brass

FIVE POINTED STAR

having its mouth closed with a stopper of lead, bearing the impression of the seal of our lord Suleyman." Most people know the story—how, by removing the seal, the fisherman let free a frightful 'Efreet. In conversation afterwards, he abjured the 'Efreet to speak the truth " By the most Great Name engraved upon the seal," and when later he persuaded the spirit to re-enter the bottle, he shut him in knowing he could not break the seal.

In the Middle Ages authors illuminated five pointed stars on the first pages of their MSS. to ensure good fortune for their work, while the other day a modern writer, who claims to be an authority on the occult, told how he used the same sign to protect himself against an elemental. Entering a house, which was reputed to be haunted, he says he at once " sensed " the presence of something evil. Taking a piece of chalk from his pocket, he drew a five pointed star on the floor and standing in the midst of it was able to bear in safety the particular haunting which had driven others insane.

In church architecture the star appears as an extra guard against the devil should he wish to enter the sacred building. A noted instance occurs in Westminster Abbey, where the beautiful west window is in the form of a pentagon. The star shown in the illustration is from an ancient frieze on the south front of Adderbury Church, Oxford.

Wizards, and all who dealt in magic, were particularly careful to have five pointed stars embroidered on their garments in order to protect themselves against any evil spirits they might raise. In " Marmion " Sir Walter Scott describes a wizard thus :—

> . . . . a quaint and fearful sight,
> His mantle lined with fox skins white;
> His high and wrinkled forehead bore
> A pointed cap, such as of yore
> Clerks say that Pharaoh's magi wore.
> His shoon were marked with cross and spell,
> Upon his breast a pentacle . . . .

In his appendix to the same poem Sir Walter quotes from " The Discourse Concerning Devils and Spirits, annexed to Reginald Scott's Discovery of Witchcraft, edition 1665 " as follows :—

" A pentacle is a piece of fine linen, folded with five corners, according to the five senses, and suitably inscribed with characters. This the magician extends towards the spirits which he invokes, when they are stubborn and rebellious, and refuse to be conformable to the ceremonies and rites of magic."

"The suitable inscriptions" were generally the signs of the planets or of the Zodiac or other sigils.

In Germany the five pointed star has been popular from the earliest times, and belief in its power as a mascot is not obsolete as many German soldiers carried charms of this shape during the Great War.

STAR SAPPHIRE

See Sapphire.

THE ORDER OF THE STAR IN THE EAST

The five pointed star is the symbol adopted by the Members of the Order of the Star in the East because—it is said—it is the sign of the Logos, and this body is in expectation of a new manifestation of the Logos in Man. A correspondent says :—

"In working on the geometry of the pentacle some years ago, I found that it is based on the Pentagon. An upright pentacle gives interiorly an inverted pentagon. Connect the points of the pentacle and you again get an upright pentagon. Prolong the sides of this pentagon and you get an inverted pentacle—and so on. It makes a series.

"In the American War of Independence, Washington went to a seamstress and gave her a 6-pointed star, with orders to place same on a flag—the inception of the U.S. flag. She took a piece of cloth and showed him that a 5-pointed star was much easier to cut out of it folded—hence the U.S. star is 5 and not 6. But I have never been able to find out how to fold a square so as easily to get a 5-pointed star out of it myself !"

SPORTSMEN (Special Mascots for)

See Amethyst.

STEPS

Talismans in the shape of steps were very popular in Egypt, and were another form of the belief in the existence of the stairway or ladder by which the spirits of the dead ascended from darkness into light. Osiris was called the god of the Staircase, that is the god by whose help souls ascended, and these mascots helped their possessors to attain lofty thoughts, to reach the heights above that which is of the earth earthy.

See also Ladder.

STONE

Almost anywhere along the coast of Britain, certainly along the East Coast, the fisher children cry out with joy if they happen to find a sea-worn stone that has a hole right through it. They take it as a sign they will have their dearest wish granted, and in many a cottage may be seen such stones put away on mantelshelf or in cupboard as bringers of good luck.

Not so very long ago it was firmly believed that one of these stones hung above the head of a bed would ensure sound sleep to those who rested there, and would dispel the evil influence of Mare, the bringer of bad dreams— the unpleasant goddess of the Norsemen whose name is remembered in our words "nightmare" and "mare's nest."

Those stones with holes in them were hung in stables also, generally being fastened round the neck or to the manger of a favourite horse. Mare was credited with a passion of midnight rides, and stablemen told of horses found lathered and trembling in the morning, because the evil spirit had been forcing them to gallop through the night.

All over the North of Scotland, and in some parts of Ireland, are stone monuments pierced with holes, and often covered with the runic inscriptions no man can read to-day. Through the holes in those old stones lovers have clasped hands through countless ages, quite sure that thus they made the keeping of their mutual troth sacred for ever.

See also Arrow and Ring.

CORONATION STONE

See Shell.

STORK

It is only necessary to read Hans Andersen to know that in Northern Europe the expression, "the stork has visited Mrs So-and-So " is equivalent to saying that that lady has had a baby.

Children in Northern Europe are told that storks bring their little brothers and sisters and drop them down the chimney, just as foolish nurses here say the new baby was dug out of the parsley bed or from under the gooseberry bush as the case may be—incidentally all these absurdities make reference to heathen mythology. The parsley and the gooseberry are " plants of Venus," and the stork was sacred to her, so the inference is not far to seek.

In Europe the storks build freely on the roofs of the houses and byres, and as they are bringers of good luck they are encouraged. In Holland and Germany the country folk says no house will be burnt down if storks build on it, while in China there is the belief that a house which harbours storks will never be visited by robbers. Storks are excellent scavengers, besides waging war on all sorts of vermin, and in times when sanitation was practically unknown, the Governors and teachers used every effort to get the people to encourage the storks.

STRAW

See Broomstick and Shinenaka.

STUDENTS (Special Mascots for)

See Angles, Ankh, and Owl.

SUN

Most of us, when we see a little charm shaped to represent the Rising Sun, think of the Australian soldiers who came amongst us during the great war, and wore the sun as their badge.

But originally the sun talisman was worn in honour of Osiris in his character of Ra, the sun god. It was the symbol of life, and thus as a mascot it gives health and success and power, particularly to those born under Leo.

SWALLOWS

Many brooches are made to represent two or three swallows in flight, and these should be powerful mascots, for swallows or martins are bringers of good fortune. When they build under the eaves of a house great prosperity may be expected, but it is important the birds should not be injured or driven away.

SWASTIKA

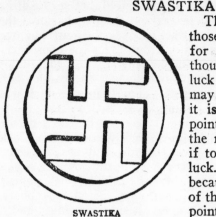

SWASTIKA

The special mascot of those who have Jupiter for their Ruling Planet, though it is a universal luck bringer, and as such may be worn by all. But it is important that the points should be turned to the right to be "lucky"; if to the left it brings ill luck. This is probably because, as it is the symbol of the Sun and of life, the points ought to follow the sun's way. All over the East the position of the points is considered most important.

The name by which we call the mascot means Happiness, and comes from the Sanscrit, the literary language of ancient India. Yet old as the name must be it is modern compared with the sign itself, for that is perhaps the oldest mascot in the world—older than the Seal of Solomon—older than the Pentagon—and at least as old as the Key of Life. It has been found engraved on stone implements belonging to the earliest races of mankind, and is on the remains of buildings raised by nations whose very names are forgotten. And it is absolutely world-wide.

On the ancient rock carvings of India it is found, it appears in the South Sea Islands, it is frequent in China and Japan—where it is the symbol of long life as well as of happiness—and appears throughout Northern Europe as the Hammer of Thor. The curious three legged sign of the Isle or Man is a form of the Swastika taken there by some very early colonist.

The Theosophic teaching about the origin of the Swastika is that it is the sign of the Infinite Life which sacrifices—crucifies—itself by coming into manifestation with the finite; hence the cross form. The outflowing life so given is symbolised by the points. In Mrs Besant's "Study of Consciousness" there is the detailed description of a series of ideas represented by a set of symbols of which the Swastika is one.

1. • the plain point alone, is Being, absolute and unconditioned.

2. ⊙ the point within the circle is Being which has chosen to manifest, to be conditioned, striking the bounds of its own limitations.

3. ✕ this point, vibrating in all directions within the limits of its sphere gives Being manifest in all planes.

4. 卐 the circle is represented now by the spinning cruciform figure with its hooks, which is the symbol of the universe within the Upholder's care.

In the Middle Ages the Swastika was frequently inscribed on church bells, particularly north of the Humber, the land in which the Danes had settled generations before. Their worship of Thor had been forgotten, yet because of some lingering tradition men saw the symbol of the Hammer as a sacred sign, and as a sort of extra protection placed it in the belfry, while they stood the Latin cross upon the altar.

TABLE OF JUPITER

An astrological talisman, worn in the Middle Ages to secure wealth, to win friendship, and to gain honour. It was formed of a thin plate of silver, that must have been made when Jupiter was in the ascendant, and on it was engraved sixteen numbers which total thirty-four—meaning 7—whichever way they are added, and surrounded by Divine names. The figures run thus :—

4	14	15	1
9	7	6	12
5	11	10	8
16	2	3	13

TALISMANIC RING

See Ring.

TAU CROSS

See Cross.

TAURUS

See Zodiac.

TAT

An Egyptian talisman, worn to give fidelity and strength, also as a key which would open all doors in this life or the life to come. Tats made of gold were placed in the coffins of the dead, protecting the soul on its journey through the underworld.

TEDDY BEAR

This is a modern invention, with no greater history behind it than the bright idea of a toy-maker in America, who produced the well-jointed figure of a woolly bear and named it Teddy in honour of Theodore Rooseveldt, then the President of the Republic. Teddy was so fascinating that he became popular everywhere, and presently appeared in the fronts of motor cars, where he was given the dignity of a mascot. Perhaps he deserved his reputation, for in many parts of the world the bear has been a powerful totem, credited with the power of bestowing good fortune, and as a mascot is the outward sign of good wishes, this queer little creature does its part when given by one friend to another. See Bear.

TEETH

Many strange legends cling to teeth, but it is difficult to trace their origins.

In some cases they are mascots, in others quite the reverse. For instance, to dream of teeth is particularly unlucky if you dream you have lost them—a belief that contradicts the familiar saying that dreams go by contrary.

A Badger's Tooth

Is the luckiest charm a gambler can carry. It should be sewn into his waistcoat pocket.

Child's First Tooth

In the North of England it is said that when the first tooth comes out, whether it has been extracted or has fallen naturally, the mother must cover it with salt and throw it on the fire, otherwise a dog's tooth will grow in its place. Probably this was some form of sacrifice to a forgotten deity.

Tiger's Tooth

In China the tiger is called the gambler's god, and his tooth is carried to ensure good fortune at any game of chance. In India the tooth of a tiger protects from ghosts of men or animals. In addition, the wearing of the tooth or claw endows with the courage and strength and cunning of the tiger himself, so that earthly foes are put to flight as well as ghostly ones.

In Monte Carlo, and similar resorts, the appearance of tiger's teeth and claws mounted in gold as charms is very frequent, which shows the idea has a wide hold still.

Wolf's Tooth.

Pliny says that the tooth of a wolf, if worn suspended horizontally round the neck of a child, was a great preventive of all teething complaints. It was worn also as a cure for toothache in adults.

TEG-A-SHIWA

A Japanese plant of which the leaves are mascots, especially for the protection of travellers. When a friend is about to start on a journey a meal is served him on these leaves instead of a plate, and after his departure the leaf from which he ate is hung over the doorway to ensure his safe return.

THUMBS UP

We all know the popular saying, and are familiar with the little Billiken-like figures in the shops. We laugh as we see the sly smile and note the clenched hand with the up-turned thumb, yet the saying comes from the Romans, with whom the position of the thumb was a matter of life or death.

Only when a man had fought bravely and well, when he had been vanquished by extreme odds or by some influence beyond his control, was " Thumbs Up " ever given. Hence while the sign means " Live on—hope on," it stands also for the reward of merit, and may be freely translated as " Keep on trying, do your best, don't show fear, and you will come out all right in the end."

TIGER

As a mascot a tiger endows with courage and strength and cunning, also he is fortunate to gamblers. See also Claws and Teeth.

TIKI

TIKI

The most important talisman of the Maoris of New Zealand, which is worn as a protection from witchcraft and is usually carved in jade, though the British Museum possesses a specimen made from a human skull. In every case the tiki is a neck ornament, and takes the form of a grotesque human figure with its head on one side as if in the act of listening. In the Museum is a jade tiki, illustrated here. The queer little creature is holding its hand to its ear in a very eloquent fashion.

TIN

Tin belongs to Sagittarius, but as a metal it does not seem to have been much used in charms or spells.

From the fact that tin ingots and manufactured articles have been found in lake dwellings we know that the metal has been used by man for thousands of years, and for an enormous length of time the Cornish tin works have been famous.

TOPAZ

It is found in many colours, though white, yellow, or pink stones are the most common, but in all its shades it has the same attributes, and as a birth stone belongs to Sagittarius.

The pink topaz only is a mascot in a secondary degree to those born under Leo.

In the Middle Ages the topaz was commonly set in gold and worn as a bracelet on the left arm as a charm against the Evil Eye—the modern bangle so often worn above the elbow might well be set with a topaz as a charming mascot. Medicinally it was a cure for asthma and gout, sleeplessness, lunacy, and sudden death, while in addition it brought riches to its wearer and the favour of great men.

TORCH

A symbol of triumphant love, of happiness, perhaps because Cupid and Hymen god of marriage, were represented carrying flaming torches.

TORTOISE

Is worn as a talisman all over the East to secure long life, and protect from the Evil Eye and Black Magic generally.

In the art of Greece and Rome the tortoise is represented accompanying the goddess of Love, the creature symbolising the feminine principle in Nature. In both China and Japan it is the talisman to secure long life, the great age to which tortoises attain being doubtless the reason why the power was assigned to it, while in the dome-like shape of its shell the ancients saw a representation of the world. Also it was a symbol of Mercury, and as such acted as a peace-maker between enemies, and a healer in cases of disease.

TOTAPHOTH

A talisman worn by the Hebrews to ensure safety on a journey, and ready hospitality from those who were to be met in strange lands. The totaphoth was a curved plate, engraved with texts from the Talmud, worn across the forehead.

Apparently the Druids wore a very similar talisman, for Boswell, in his additions to Camden, describing a thin, crescent-shaped plate of gold which had been dug up in an Irish bog says:—

"Mr Vallancey determines them to be ornaments of the Hibernian Druids, representing the moon in the first quarter, whence the name Cead Raire. They were carried by the Druids in their hands when they went to cut mistletoe, as represented on a bas relief found at Autum in Auberi's antiquities of that place."

Those last words suggest that these crescents may have

been some form of the "golden knives" with which Cæsar tells us the Druids were in the habit of cutting the mistletoe.

TOTEM

The totem, which remains to-day in the grotesque carvings of the Maoris, the crude clay figures of the Central African, and the strange signs daubed on the tepis of North American Indians, is one of the oldest of all mascots.

In far pre-historic times man began to divide into families, or tribes, and as his power of language grew, it was necessary for him to devise means by which these tribes could be distinguished from each other. Gradually each took to itself a sign, choosing some animal or plant and—to quote Lang's "Custom and Myth":—"When these small groups had received . . . names—and had forgotten how or why—they argued, as savages always do, that there was a mystic and potent connection between each group and its name-giving animal."

Thus, though at first the totem was merely a distinguishing mark, as the brain of man developed, the instinct of veneration stirred in his waking soul. He groped for God and, in his darkness, worshipped the totem which bound him to his brothers, giving him the comfort of comradeship and understanding.

Long after totem worship had been forgotten in ancient Egypt, many villages kept this or that animal as sacred— a lingering remnant of the older religion, though another had come to take its place. In one village no crocodile must be hurt, in another the ibis was protected, in a third the cat was sacred, and so on; and from the same old faith probably came the custom of endowing certain of gods with the heads of animals.

TOURMALINE

Second perhaps only to amber, the tourmaline is charged with electricity. It is a semi-transparent crystal which is found in all shades and colours, often made into beads. As a mascot it should be worn by actors, artistes, authors, poets, musicians, and the like, to attract inspiration, and as a birth stone it belongs to Leo.

TRAVELLERS (Special Mascots for)

See Amber, Caul, Day, Emerald, Jet, Moonstone, Shell, Solomon's Seal.

TRUMPET OF VICTORY

Is one of the Eight Glorious Emblems of Buddha, and as such brings lofty thoughts and divine inspiration. Also it inspires courage, and leads to hope and ultimate success.

TURQUOISE

The birth stone of Taurus.

Its blue colour dedicates this stone to Venus, thus it is the mascot of lovers and married people. It is more used for mascots than any other stone, and until quite modern times was believed to have power of warning its wearer of danger by changing its colour. It is recorded that King John had warning of his approaching death by seeing the blue turquoise in his ring turn to dull green. In these cases the change of colour was temporary. With age, or after being washed with soap, practically all turquoises become green, but that change is very different from the one which warns.

In the East it is called the horseman's talisman, protecting from falls and injuries received while riding, and in the Middle Ages it renewed friendships, healed quarrels, thwarted enemies, and prevented headache.

TUSK

An important mascot in itself, a bringer of general good fortune, yet chiefly prized because it has the power of strengthening the influence of all other mascots. Tusks were attached to necklaces and bangles and religious symbols that the good influence of those mascots and amulets might be increased.

TWISTED ROOTS

This is a Romany belief which was told the writer by a gipsy in the New Forest. If in your travels you find a twisted root that is coiled into the shape of the letter " J " or " S " take it home and set great store by it. Should you touch a person with it on the hand or the face, that person will be obliged to do your bidding, to stay with you or to go away exactly as you may wish.

UMBRELLA

A Hindu mascot of great power, bringing universal good fortune, venerated as one of the Eight Glorious Emblems of Buddha.

Umbrellas are a modern invention so far as England is concerned, for it was not until somewhere about the reign of Queen Anne that they became fashionable. They were described in the dictionaries of the time as " portable pent houses to carry in a person's hand as screen from violent rain or heat," but it was taken for granted only women would avail themselves of the shelter. One of the very early magazines published for ladies, " The Female Tatler," of December 12th, 1709, has a sneer at a young gentleman who borrowed his sweetheart's umbrella, while John Macdonald, a footman, who wrote his autobiography in the eighteenth century, says he possessed :—" A fine silk umbrella brought from Spain but could not with any comfort to myself use it, the people calling out, ' Frenchman, why don't you get a coach? ' " However he persisted for three months, and by that time the public seemed to have grown accustomed to his eccentricity, for he adds they " took no notice of this novelty. Foreigners began to use theirs, and then the English."

The credit of introducing umbrellas to England is generally given to Jonas Hanway, a brave man and a great philanthropist, who carried his umbrella in the face of all opposition and did a great deal more to popularise it than would have been possible for the footman.

In the East the umbrella has been part of the insignia of royalty, a symbol of state and power since very early times. It was evolved from the canopy of state of which it remains a form.

In many parts of England you will hear that it is unlucky to open an umbrella in a house or to lay one on a table, and old actors declared no good fortune would come to a drama if an open umbrella or sunshade were carried on the stage. But in view of modern theatrical productions this tradition seems to be forgotten.

VASE

One of the Eight Glorious Emblems of Buddha, and a bringer of good fortune. Mascots in this shape are particularly powerful to those born under Aquarius, which see.

VIRGO

See Zodiac.

VULTURE

In Egypt mascots made in the likeness of this very unpleasant bird were worn to protect from the bites of scorpions and to attract love, in memory of the belief that when the god Horus was stung to death by a scorpion his mother, Isis, disguised herself as a vulture and flew to and fro seeking him. Thoth, stirred to pity by her bitter grief, gave her the " words of wisdom "—shall we translate that as knowledge of the antidote?—by which her son was restored to life.

WAGTAIL

The gipsies call the wagtail the Romany bird, and have the strange belief that if you meet a wagtail on the road you will see a true born Romany before many minutes have passed. As a mascot the little creature has the power of granting any wish which may be in the mind of the person across whose path it flies.

WEDDING (Special Mascots for)

See Aquamarine, Beryl, Colour, Confetti, Knife, Knot, Lodestone, Myrtle, Rice, Ring, Rosemary, and Shoes.

WHEEL

Worn to secure good fortune, or rather change of fortune when it is bad, so that the ill luck may pass and good luck rise with the turn of wheel, also (in India) to win success in law suits.

In Greek and Roman mythology the goddess Fortuna was represented holding a wheel as a symbol of inconstancy, but Buddha gave the wheel a more sacred significance. Seated in a rice field he drew the Wheel of Life on the ground with grains of rice, in order to illustrate his teaching that cause and effect follow each other throughout creation as by the turning of a wheel.

The Wheel of the Law was one of his Eight Glorious Emblems, and a very powerful talisman.

The tyre of a wheel represented Eternity—it was another form of the coiled snake—in many religions, and to the Druids, who used wheels in their most solemn divinations, the hub was the symbol of the sun, the spokes represented the planets revolving about it, and the tyre was the emblem of Eternity.

In many shops little wheel charms may be bought, generally with miniature handles fixed round the tyre so that they resemble the steering wheel of a ship. These are a modern addition. The original wheel, worn for good luck, had no such handles.

WHEEL CROSS
See Cross.

WHITE HEATHER
See Heather.

WISHBONE
See Merrythought.

WITCHCRAFT (to Prevent)
See Evil Eye.

WOLF
A wolf hardly seems a promising mascot, yet to see a wolf or to have one cross the path is very fortunate, and ornaments made in the likeness of wolves keep bad luck out of the house. Apparently the idea is that while not bringing actual good fortune they drive evil influences away. In the third book of " Notable Things " there appears :—

" Pliny reports that men in ancient times did fasten upon the gates of their towns, the heads of wolves, thereby to put away witchery, sorcery, or enchantment."
See Teeth.

WREN
The little wren is almost as powerful a mascot as the robin, with which it is linked in the old rhyme :—

Cock Robin, Jenny Wren,
God Almighty's cock and hen.

As in so many other cases probably this doggerel is a phonetic attempt to repeat words of another language, words whose meaning would be utterly different if it could be known. In folk-lore the robin is always male and the wren female—the nursery rhyme Who Killed Cock Robin? is a case in point—and both birds bring good fortune, providing no harm is done to them and their nests are not disturbed.

WOMEN (Special Mascots for)

As Isis in ancient Egypt was the Universal Mother, the protectress of women and of all young creatures, so in later years this guardianship passed to Diana, who was another form of Isis. Diana was so horrified at seeing the result of child-birth pain that she vowed perpetual chastity, but begged that Jove would allow her to be the guardian of other women in their time of trial. Her prayer was granted : thus all mascots for women attract the influence of Isis in one of her many forms, but chiefly in that of Diana.

See Arrowhead, Coral, Crescent, Cybele, Dock, Eggs, Emerald, Lizard, Mandrake, and Moon.

ZIRCON

See Jacinth.

ZODIAC

In the earliest ages astrology was the recognised religion of primeval man, and the beliefs taught in those past æons have not been absolutely blotted out to-day. Indeed most thinkers have come to agree there is some germ of mighty truth lying in the tissue of superstition with which the science has been embroidered by ignorance and charlatanism. To put the case quite crudely, quite unscientifically, as we talk of those in the south being "hot blooded," of those nearer the pole coming from the colder North, and thus being slower in their passions, so the position of the sun and the planets at the time of birth has influence over a child, and his or her nature is in harmony with those influences.

It is easy to test the truth or otherwise of such a statement. Read the characteristics astrology gives to those born in certain periods and compare them with the characters of those of your acquaintance whose birth dates you know, or with the celebrated people whose names figure in

Whitaker's Almanack. It is not suggested that every child born in a given period must have all the characteristics fully developed—allowance has to be made for other influences and for the fact that there is no hard and fast line dividing the separate Houses—thus the influence of the preceding sign is felt at the beginning of the next, just as the influence of the following sign becomes evident towards the end.

Planetary influences again must be considered. The position of any planet which happened to be in the sky at the time of birth is important, as these modify or intensify the influence of the House.

How the Heavens Were Mapped Into Houses

When the shepherds of Chaldea first reduced their ancient study of the heavens into something like mathematical exactitude, they realised the sun made a complete circle of the heavens, returning to what may be called the starting place in the spring when its rays gathered power. For purposes of calculation they divided the heavens—the " sky " shall we say?—into twelve parts or divisions, which they called Houses, and thus they formed their year which was divided into twelve parts, coinciding with the stay of the sun in one or other of those divisions.

These twelve Houses were not the same as our months; the latter are of infinitely later date, hence there arises confusion when any attempt is made to fix birth date influences according to our present calendar. For instance, the familiar booklets which give this or that " birth day luck " for those " born in April " are misleading. April does not exist astrologically. For the first twenty-one days of the month the sun is in Aries, and for the rest of the time in Taurus, the influences varying accordingly.

Each Sign in the Zodiac—as the Twelve Houses are called—has a name which is typical of those born under its influence. The question will arise—Were the names given because the people of the sign showed these resemblances, or do the people develop along certain lines because of the name?

Cold common sense will suggest an answer, and surely that is the right one. The ancients were students of psychology as well as of astrology, and in choosing the name of the Sign they considered the results of its influences.

Here, then, is a brief account of the Signs of the Zodiac, the names which have become their symbols, and the characteristics of those born during their periods. The " lucky colours, jewels, metals, days, numbers," have been dealt with already in full detail. See under separate heads.

THE HOUSE OF ARIES THE RAM

The sun is in this house from March 21st to April 20th, approximately. Ruling planet Mars.

In all early religions the ram was the emblem of sacrifice, and from sacrifice sprang blessing and success as harvest follows the sowing of the seed. Thus when the Chaldeans fixed this period of spring as the beginning of their year it was natural they should choose the ram as the symbol of the period—the ram of sacrifice, from whose blood all blessings were to come.

In the Old Testament there are many references to the ram of sacrifice—Abraham seeing the ram caught in the thicket by its horns when he was about to offer up his son is a case in point—" the ram of the atonement " is mentioned in Numbers—at the institution of the Passover, Moses was commanded to sacrifice a young ram—and in Micah we find the cry—" Will the Lord be pleased with thousands of rams or with ten thousand rivers of oil? " Thus insinuating that rams and oil were the most acceptable of sacrifices.

People born at this season are pioneers, they seldom care to serve under others, but want to lead in all they undertake. They have keen intellects, but are impulsive and apt to say more than they mean, though they are ever ready to fight the battles of those they think wrongly oppressed. The women will be excellent managers, and therefore make good wives, but they are inclined to be " the grey mares that are the better horses." However, all Aries people are faithful in love and friendship, and capable of deep affection though inclined to jealousy.

They resemble the ram in a tendency to butt through all obstruction, and must beware of obstinacy and of a reluctance to own when they are in the wrong, while those born during the last ten days are almost sure to be head-strong and difficult to govern.

Many Aries people are extremely successful in business and others have become great philanthropists. But whatever the career chosen it should be one in which their individual powers have a chance of developing—they are not good at mere routine. They will find their most sympathetic friends amongst those born under Leo or Sagittarius, though the people of Gemini and Aquarius have much in common with them also. On the other hand, they will have little sympathy with those of Cancer or Capricorn.

It is said that Aries people born in the morning will be more fortunate than those born later in the day.

The harmonious colour is red, the fortunate number 1, diamond and bloodstone are the gems, and iron is the metal. Any business connected with iron is sure to bring them success. Tuesday is their fortunate day.

The House of Taurus the Bull

The sun enters this House on April 21st and leaves it on May 22nd, approximately. Ruling planet Venus.

In ancient Egypt the sacred bull, Apis, was worshipped as the symbol of fecundity, and the priests taught that when their great god Osiris was murdered by Typhon his soul passed into an ox, probably because during the earthly reign of Osiris and Isis the Egyptians were taught the science of agriculture, and the ox was the animal by whose strength the ploughs were drawn and the soil was tilled. A sacred ox was kept in the Egyptian temples, and when he died the nation mourned afresh for Osiris, while every year, in the spring when the Sun is in the House of Taurus, a seven days' festival was held in honour of the bull.

This worship of the bull—or rather this seeing a

reminder of the god in a bull—spread wide. Probably the sacred cattle of the Hindus are an off-shoot of the same faith.

Before this sign was given the name of Taurus, it seems to have been known as Te—a word meaning the foundation, and it was while the sun was in this House that the foundation of the two Jewish temples were laid—probably most of the mighty buildings of antiquity were begun at the same period for the same reason.

Taurus people have many of the characteristics of the bull : they are patient, obstinate—especially if born at the beginning of the period—plodding and persevering. Yet as Osiris was wedded to Isis, so Taurus is ruled by Venus, and you will find in Taurus folk a deep love of the beautiful and artistic, and a passionate devotion to all young things—a direct attribute from the mother goddess.

A love of animals is a strong characteristic, or perhaps an interest in them would be a better word, and often these people will be found to possess a curious, almost hypnotic power over the most savage brutes which become docile with them.

To an extent the influences of Venus and Taurus are conflicting : thus Venus gives idleness and irresponsibility, a tendency to take the line of least resistance, to be easily influenced—often led astray—by those they happen to admire.

On the other hand, Taurus gives a power of concentration, and though its people are slow to forget and forgive and are apt to nurse the memory of any wrong, they are very faithful friends.

But as a rule both influences mingle to modify each other, though one or other is the stronger in different subjects. Thus Venus gives artistic ability while Taurus endows with shrewd common sense. You will find many artists and musicians born under this sign, but all have the business ability which enables them to make their art profitable.

Those born during the first ten days of the sign will have this practical side more fully developed than the others, but it is to be found in all to a greater or less degree.

Success in any business connected with speculation or on the Stock Exchange is one of the gifts of the period, while in addition the Taurus people are interested in chemistry, building, and forms of agriculture such as floriculture or fruit growing. The women are good cooks.

They are the most difficult people to lead : they are too headstrong for that, and yet are easily influenced—a seeming paradox, yet a truth.   They are frequently spendthrifts, never valuing money for its own sake, but only for what it will buy.   Usually they are ardent lovers and have many love affairs.   Frequently they are married twice.

To keep in good health they need to lead very active lives; any sedentary occupation is bad for them in every way.

Those born between sunset and midnight will never be able to keep money, though those born after midnight and before sunrise may attain wealth. It is very fortunate for a Taurus baby to be born on a Friday, since Friday is the particular day of the sign.   Their metal is copper, their stones sapphire and turquoise, 6 is their fortunate number, and their colour is blue, though violet is harmonious also.   In a secondary degree the opal is fortunate and so is coral, but neither the jacinth nor the garnet should be worn.

Taurus people will be most likely to find sympathy and understanding amongst those born under Cancer, Virgo, Capricorn, or Pisces.

THE HOUSE OF GEMINI THE TWINS

May 22nd to June 21st approximately.   Ruling planet Mercury.

A frequent and very ancient symbol of this sign was two pillars joined at the top and the base, and we are told that outside the temple of Solomon, but quite distinct from it, the great king raised two pillars, of which the one was called " Jachin," i.e., " He will establish," and the other " Boaz "—" In Him is strength."   In the East it is the custom still to raise a sort of arch or gateless gateway, if the term may be allowed, in front of the temples, probably the custom dating to some now forgotten belief which was in the mind of Solomon.

The other and more familiar symbol of the sign shows two children embracing each other, and these are taken to represent Castor and Pollux, the twin sons of Jupiter and Leda, whom he wooed in the shape of a swan. When they grew up the youths became great adventurers, and sailed with Jason in his quest of the golden fleece. During the voyage a storm threatened to wreck the ship, when flames of fire—or halos—were seen around the heads of the twins and the storm ceased. From that time they were hailed as the patrons of navigation, while it is a fact that there are fewer storms at this season than at any other.

Castor was killed in a brawl, and inconsolable for his loss Pollux prayed Jupiter he might share his brother's fate. The god granted the prayer in a curious way—for six years they alternately lived and died every day—or every six months according to some authorities—the one being ever amongst the mournful gloom of Hades, while the other was on earth.

In the end Jupiter carried them both to the heavens and made them the constellation we know as Castor and Pollux, but even the two never appear together—as the one rises the other sets. From this it is not difficult to draw the conclusion that the stars were given their names long, long before the legend of the two brothers had its birth, and that the whole is a parable to illustrate the rising and setting of the constellations.

In Roman times there were many legends that ghostly figures of Castor and Pollux, armed with spears and wearing golden helmets, each topped by a glittering star, had appeared to lead armies to victory—a very old, old version of the story of the Angels of Mons.

Keeping those legends in mind will help towards an understanding of the characters of those born under this dual sign.

Gemini people are extremely talented in two different directions so that they have difficulty in deciding to which career they should devote themselves, and it is seldom they follow one business or profession throughout their lives. They are educated for one and make an attempt at it—often a successful attempt—then drift into something quite different.

They take up new interests very quickly, and are apt to tire of their surroundings or their friends when the first novelty has worn off, yet when their affections are once fixed they are all enduring.

As they have generally a flow of language and are quick to grasp both sides of a question they make good lawyers, lecturers or teachers. Clerical work suits them, and as dramatic ability is another of the gifts, many actors and journalists are born under the sign. An aptitude for learning languages is theirs and that is fortunate since they are always restless and travel calls them constantly. Many become clever detectives, in fact they are distinctly people of the sort that are governed by the head rather than the heart.

They should guard against hardness of disposition and a lack of sympathy with others, and if they give way to their besetting sins they will become cunning and cruel. Crimes of violence or of sudden passion will not be their temptation, but the gentlemanly swindler, the clever adventuress, the bogus company promoter—those are Gemini people when the gifts have turned to evil.

Always they make many friends by their fascination of manner, and if bad luck comes they have some unexpected resource which enables them to meet it. But above all other people they should think before they act, and even when they feel they have made a mistake in any grave matter, such as the choice of a career, they should not start afresh until they have weighed all the pros and cons.

Those born at the early part of the period will have more indecision than the others. As the sign progresses the power of concentration develops.

Taurus, Virgo, or Pisces people are not likely to be in harmony with those of Gemini—they will find more congenial companionship amongst those of Libra and

Aquarius—also with those of Aries and Leo, though in a smaller degree.

Their fortunate number is 5, the agate and the crysoprase are their stones, while some authorities add the beryl. Wednesday is their fortunate day, and silver their metal. Their harmonious colour is silvery white, and they will find Solomon's Seal their special mascot.

All Gemini people should guard against their natural inclination to worry, and should take sufficient rest. Generally they have the tendency to turn night into day, and to overtax their powers.

THE HOUSE OF CANCER THE CRAB

Entered by the sun June 22nd and occupied till July 23rd approximately. Ruling planet the Moon.

Most antiquarians hold that the crab is another form of the Egyptian scarab or beetle, and in considering the characteristics of those who come under its influence it is as well to turn back to what has been written already about that persevering little creature. On the other hand, it has been said that in the name which was given to the sign in prehistoric times we have proof of the astronomical knowledge of the ancients. When the Sun enters this sign it has reached the limit of its northern declination, therefore it appears to remain stationary for a few days and then to go backwards, and the fact that a crab moves sideways is supposed to have led to the creature being selected as emblematic of the sun at this period of the year.

Yet the Greeks—embroidering on the earlier stories—had a legend that the crab was placed in the heavens by Juno in gratitude for an attack made by it upon Hercules who had offended the goddess.

Children born under the Sign are extremely sensitive, and will only thrive if they are given cheerful surroundings with plenty of fresh air and sunshine. The sea calls them, many sailors are born at this period, and so are boys who want to run away to sea even if they do not do so. Often Cancer people are so shy as to appear actually timid, but the longing for great adventure lies beneath the surface.

Many ups and downs in life await them. Often they lose all they have gained and have to start life afresh, but they are persevering; when once they take hold of anything they seldom loose their grip—a very crab-like attribute—and thus gain their goal. They should avoid speculation and games of chance, for luck seldom befriends them. Whatever they gain is by sheer dogged work. They are loyal to their friends and relations, quite clannish indeed, but are subject to moods which make them seem changeable in their likes and dislikes, and they must guard against fits of black depression. Poetry and music are amongst the gifts of the sign, and they do well as collectors of rare and valuable articles or in historical research. When trust is reposed in them they prove very reliable but are apt to resent interference. Often they have to suffer unjustly for the sins of others.

They seldom prosper early in life. With the passing of years they gain experience and are wise enough to benefit by it.

Stinginess is a weakness they have to guard against, though economy is one of their virtues. Always they are over anxious where money is concerned, and if they give way to their weakness they become misers. They are inclined to be mean over trifles, even when they are generous in larger things.

Those born towards the end of the period will be the best in every way, for the influence of Leo will soften and counteract the faults of Cancer.

Cancer people will be most in sympathy with those of their own sign or of Scorpio, Capricorn, or Pisces. Their special talisman is the scarab, their fortunate stone the emerald, the moonstone, or the pearl, though cat's eyes and crystals are lucky to them also. Any shade of green is their colour, but apart from that they should choose only light shades. The metal is silver, and the numbers are 2 and 7.

The House of Leo the Lion

The sun enters this House on July 23rd, approximately, and leaves it about August 23rd. Ruling planet the Sun.

The ancients worshipped the sun in many forms, and amongst them was that of a lion, the idea being that in its intense heat the sun scorched up and laid waste the lands as a raging lion might in his fury. The Egyptians kept approximately our month of July sacred to the lion, whence it is easy to understand why they gave his name to this portion of the heavens, while the Greeks told that the lion was a fabled monster of Nemea who was slain by Hercules. The hero clothed himself in the creature's skin which he wore ever afterwards, thus apparently securing some of the lion's attributes—the story of Elisha wearing the mantle of Elijah is of the same type.

Long before the Greeks told of Hercules—before the Egyptians worshipped the sun as the lion—this part of the heavens was given the name of the King of Beasts. And as it is nearest the zenith and the sun's heat is greatest when it is in Leo, it is easy to realise why it is the symbol of power.

"Lion-hearted" is an excellent description of its people. They are full of courage, have enormous vitality and influence over others. They are generous to a fault, loving, quick-tempered, yet ready to forget and forgive injury. It was the Leo people who faced martyrdom un-flinchingly, for they are enthusiasts—whatever their religion they are ready to die for it, just as they will risk all and sacrifice all for the sake of those they love.

Light and warmth and colour are necessary to them, yet though they love gay surroundings and merry music they are in no sense frivolous, indeed they have grave and serious thoughts for higher things. They are seldom successful in trade, buying and selling is not for them, but the arts appeal, especially any form of decoration. They excel as dress designers, as furnishers, as landscape gardeners, in fact, in any trade where their excellent tastes can have full play, but also they are fitted for a career which will benefit their fellow-men. Of all people those of Leo at its best, wish to leave the world better than they found it.

In money matters they are fortunate, and yet because of their generosity they seldom save, and are on the verge of poverty often, but when things are at their worst Fortune's wheel generally turns and all is well again. Travel is not fortunate for them, they will not succeed in any career which needs frequent change of scene.

When the evil influences of the sign develop they become arrogant, boastful, self-indulgent, and reckless, and are possessed by a love of notoriety which will lead them to plunge into any sort of folly in order to attract attention. In a word, they must be in the limelight, and do not stop to count the cost. They are extravagant in every sense of the word.

With the people of Cancer, Scorpio, or Pisces, they are not likely to be in agreement, but should look for companionship amongst those of Aries, Sagittarius, or Aquarius, though at times the people of Leo can " agree to differ " with those of the opposing signs, and then very true friendships or deep loves result.

Golden colour—the colour of the sun—is harmonious to Leo people, though green is fortunate, also as is white. Yellow stones and most green ones are fortunate, but amber is their special mascot. Their fortunate day is Sunday.

The House of Virgo, the Virgin

The sun enters this House about August 24th and leaves it approximately on September 22nd. Ruling planet is Mercury.

The symbol of this sign has been identified with Ceres, goddess of Plenty; with Isis, the mother; with the Holy Virgin, yet a very little knowledge brings us to the fact that for the purposes of the symbol all are the same— they stand for the Eternal, the Holy Mother.

Mr Pavitt, in his " Book of Talismans," says :—" It is worthy of note that the founder of the ancient city of Paris believed in the power and influence of the heavenly bodies, it (the city) being named by an old astrologer Para-Isis, meaning in Phœnician The Star of Being or Existence. Corroboration of this can been seen at the present day in Notre Dame Cathedral where, amongst the twelve signs of the Zodiac engraved on the outside when entering from the north, the sixth sign has been represented by the figure of the Virgin elevated above all the rest. It was also in the sixth month that the Annunciation took place."

This then is the House dedicated to the Eternal Mother, the bringer forth of life, the guardian in whose arms all new born creatures rest, yet the power of Mercury is strong also, so that the people of this House seem to have dual characters, and are difficult to understand. They are reserved and cold in manner, often they are called sly, yet as a matter of fact they are extremely honest, most reliable in business and thoroughly practical.

All born under the sign are absolutely undemonstrative, yet in their hearts is hidden a deep power of affection, and a craving to love and to be loved. When they marry they are devoted partners and parents. A Virgo man will work day and night for wife and home, and a Virgo woman will have her home clean as the proverbial new pin and excellently ordered. Their great fault lies in a tendency to worry over trifles, which is apt to make them trying companions, and because of their natural respect for law and order they are stern in their judgment of others who fall.

They succeed in any occupation that requires accuracy and method instead of inspiration, hence they are excellent teachers and clerks, while often they do well as farmers, chemists, or photographers.

They seldom grow rich suddenly : when success comes it has been earned by hard work and dogged perseverance. They travel a good deal, change their homes often, and may expect their best fortune after they have passed the age of forty.

Mention has been made of the fact that Virgo people have little mercy on sinners, and yet when these people are tempted and fall—a somewhat rare occurence—they " go the whole hog " as the eloquent if not very refined phrase has it. If once they cross the boundary they sink to the lowest depths. There can be no half measure.

Their metal is silver, their colour silvery grey, their stone jade or cornelian, which must be set in silver or platinum, not in gold. Their fortunate day is Tuesday.

Yellow is a colour they should avoid, and all yellow stones in particular.

The House of Libra, the Balance

The sun enters this House about September 23rd and leaves it on October 23rd. Ruling planets Venus and Saturn.

It is believed that in the very old Zodiacs—those of a prehistoric period—this House was called by another name which meant an altar. Certainly in ancient writings it is called Tul-ku, meaning Holy Altar, and the Bible tells us that in both the first and the second temples the altar was dedicated in the seventh month—this is the Seventh House of the Zodiac, and the name of our month September, which is practically coincident with it, means seven.

The oldest historic mention of the House is Egyptian, and there it is named The Yoke—that is the beam of the scales only. In this form it typified an instrument used for measuring the rising of the Nile.

People born under this sign are sweet tempered and level-headed—they " hold the balance " truly, and weigh up the pros and cons of any question before they act. They are resourceful and clever, never more happy than when they are working for others, and the simple life appeals to them. They may enjoy creature comforts—who does not?—but they care nothing for position or rank. It is said the percentage of happy marriages is larger amongst Libra people than those of any other sign, yet they are extremely sensitive, and when wounded by one they love the hurt goes deep.

Because of the strong sense of justice many great lawyers and judges have been born under this sign, but decorative work appeals to Libra people in every form. Love of books and flowers is another characteristic, invariably they have great taste in arranging the latter. In fact they are artistic in the best sense of the word, and work for sheer love of art instead of for the money or fame it may bring them.

They are intensely sympathetic, responding to influences around them, and often this gift is intensified to clairvoyance. It has been said that all Libra people are clairvoyant, though the gift may remain undeveloped.

" Luck " seldom favours them, thus they should leave all forms of gambling alone. They are often fortunate in speculation, but that is because they have great forethought and have reckoned out the possibilities correctly. As a rule they have many ups and downs in life, and know both poverty and wealth.

Their fortunate day is Friday, their number 6, and their jewels the opal and coral with the lapis lazuli second. Blue is their colour, but violet will be harmonious also, though they should avoid very dark purple or black, and as with Taurus people they will find the Seal of Solomon is their special mascot. Their best chance of companionship lies with those born under Aquarius, Gemini, or their own sign.

THE HOUSE OF SCORPIO, THE SCORPION

The sun enters this House approximately on October 24th and leaves it on November 23rd. Ruling planet Mars.

Probably if this were called the " House of the Serpent " the name would be more correct, for the sign seems connected with serpent worship, perhaps the oldest known religion—the religion whose influence is to be traced through so many other faiths.

In proof of this in some old Zodiacs this House is simply called " The Oldest," but in Greek mythology it is named after the Scorpion who killed the giant Orion.

According to the legend Orion in his strength boasted there was not a creature on earth he could not subdue, when a scorpion, crawing on the ground, stung him fatally in the foot. Another story goes that the scorpion acted by command of Juno—or Diana—whom the giant had offended, and that in reward for the deed the creature was placed amongst the stars as a constellation. The same fate—or reward—was given to Orion and his dog. The stars bearing the name of the giant and his faithful friend are the most familiar of all in the heavens.

There are few weak characters born under the sign,

for whether for good or ill Scorpio people are the sort of whom we may say they are good friends but bad enemies. They pay their debts—generally with interest.

The gift of healing is strong—and healing has been connected with "the wisdom of the serpent" from the earliest times. Good doctors and nurses are found amongst Scorpio people, and all take an interest in medicine and in the course of illnesses. As public speakers they have the power of swaying those who hear them—as reformers they are heart and soul with the Cause with which they are identified—as authors they will write books with a purpose—and they succeed as school teachers because they are good organisers and are more fitted to lead others than to serve. Any form of engineering or any occupation connected with electricity or chemistry will suit them also.

In order to get on in the world they must have the incentive of ambition—or the wish to succeed for the sake of others. Failing that the worst side of their nature is apt to rise and much of what has just been written will be negatived.

Scorpio represents the serpent—and like sleeping serpents the passions of jealousy and revenge lie in the hearts of Scorpio people ready to wake into dangerous life unless kept under control.

In a recently published article on astrology the following occurred :—

"Love is capable of stirring all that is best and all that is worst in the Scorpio nature to activity. It is not at all uncommon for a man who has been known to his friends and family as a persevering student and worker, to change completely because of some violent and sudden infatuation. Actually he has not changed. He has had the latent passions in his disposition called to life. He gives himself up to bad influences and goes from bad to worse till he sinks to the depths.

"Or a girl, whose life has been innocent and peaceful suddenly finds a lover in some worthless man. She falls beneath a temptation which no one imagined could come to such as she seemed. Or she is jilted and the once gentle nature becomes vindictive. cruel, and capable of any wickedness in her thirst for revenge.

"Such are extreme cases, but they may serve as examples. The best and worst of all dispositions may lie dormant till some sudden event calls them to life, but in few are the opposing elements so strong as they are in the Scorpio people. Those who learn to subdue and conquer their passions are amongst the saints of this world. As their temptations are great so are their victories."

Scorpio people are devoted husbands and wives and good parents, but they want to rule the roost at home as in business, and often this characteristic will bring disaster unless it is curbed.

Their best chance of happiness lies with those born under their own sign or under Taurus, Cancer, or Pisces, but they should beware of those born under Aries, Leo, or Sagittarius. Also astrology is emphatic in declaring that the numbers, jewels, colours, etc., which are fortunate to the three last named signs, will be absolutely tragic in their influences on Scorpio people.

Their fortunate day is Tuesday, their number is 9, their stones the aquamarine or beryl, the lodestone and the carbuncle. But all red stones are fortunate, red being their harmonious colour.

Their special talisman is a ring or bracelet in the form of a serpent.

SAGITTARIUS, THE HOUSE OF THE ARCHER
November 23rd to December 21st.
Ruling planet Jupiter.

The symbol of the House is a Centaur armed with his bow and arrow, and in the heavens three stars represent the weapon. It was the Greeks who first adopted the Centaur to represent this House, and according to them he was Chiron, the son of Saturn and Philyra, whom Saturn had wooed in the shape of a horse. When her child was born Philyra was so horrified at its monstrosity that she begged the gods to take her from earth, and was duly transformed into a lime—or linden—tree which was called by her name in Greek.

Meanwhile Chiron took to the woods and there devoted himself to the study of herbs and the stars. As a consequence he became celebrated as a physician, people flocked to consult him, while because of his scientific knowledge he was appointed tutor to the young heroes of the day. Hercules, Achilles, Jason and practically all the other great warriors of mythology were said to have learnt from Chiron, while Esculapius, first of physicians, was his pupil also.

Chiron was not the only Centaur in the world, there was a whole tribe of these half men, half horses in Thessaly, and against these Hercules carried on war. Seeing Chiron in the distance he mistook him for a foe and shot an arrow which wounded him in the knee. Frantic with remorse Hercules tried to save his old tutor, but Chiron begged Jupiter to release him from his agonies and was thereupon translated to the heavens, and placed amongst the stars under the name of Sagittarius.

This is considered a very fortunate time of the year in which to be born, for whatever troubles come to Sagittarius people Jupiter is watching over them ready to help, as the god released the centaur from his pain. Again, the bow is another form of the rainbow, always the symbol of hope.

The people of Sagittarius are full of hope, they make many friends, and are quick-witted, clear-sighted and resourceful—as an archer must be. They have energy and determination, and while they do not interfere with others they are ready to resent interference with themselves.

As a rule travel is not fortunate, yet it is often their fate to take long journeys and to settle in a foreign land. They should beware of accidents, particularly those caused by animals, though they are very fond of all dumb creatures and have considerable power over them.

One of their great faults is that they are exacting. They would be a great deal more happy if they were more ready to make allowance for others, and they must beware of a tendency to fault finding and selfishness and to taking offence where none is meant. They hate to be ruled, and though they like companionship and love to be surrounded by others, do not like working under a master. They are extremely impulsive, to them the old marry-in-haste-re-pent-at-leisure proverb often applies. But they have great determination, and when they have taken up any cause or profession will work at it till they drop.

Unfortunately their impulsiveness often leads them to give up one career and take up another, in fact at their worst the Sagittarius people never seem to be in the same mind two days together.

They generally have many love affairs and often marry twice, while some important event or change of fortune marks their thirtieth year.

Many musicians are born under this sign, and they make good church workers, preachers, lecturers, or teachers, and do well in almost any career that takes them into the open air.

They will find their best chances of congenial companionship with those born under Aries, Gemini, Leo, or their own sign. In a secondary degree, they would probably get on well with those of Aquarius or Libra. With the people of Pisces, Cancer, or Scorpio they are quite likely to feel strong superficial attraction—a mutual fascination as it were—and though life-long friendships and happy marriages might result, there would always be a wide difference of thought, an essential antagonism between the two natures.

Sagittarius people will find three is their number, Thursday their day, and either the topaz or the crysolite their jewel, though some authorities give the amethyst as well. Certainly purple is their colour, and tin their metal.

The House of Capricorn, the Goat

The sun enters this House on or about December 22nd and leaves it again January 19. Ruling planet Saturn.

Saturn plays a very important part in this House, so much so that in some of the old Zodiacs the figure we call Father Time is used to denote it instead of the goat—Father Time being Saturn. The fact that the shortest day falls during this period is worthy of note.

In Greek the two words " Time " and " Saturn " are the same save for one letter, so the confusion between them or rather their actual identity is easy to understand. The ancient Greeks considered their god Pan, with his goat's legs and hoofs—the "cloven hoof "of the Christian idea of Satan—was the deity represented by this House, and their zodiacs showed the goat with the hind quarters of a fish because of the legend that when Pan was attacked by Typhon—otherwise Saturn—on the banks of the Nile, he plunged into the river, changing himself into a monster.

The people of Capricorn are seldom destined to be rich, as the goat lives on bare mountain tops and subsists on scanty herbage, so they lead hard and struggling lives. But they are plodding and painstaking, sure footed in every sense of the word, and thanks to the influence of Saturn after middle age their lives will be much more comfortable and successful than in their youth. When they succeed—as some do most brilliantly—it is by sheer perseverance and hard work. Always they are steadfast and faithful to their ideals, but often love of money may make them self-centred and selfish, and always they are very apt to be despondent and to look on the dark side of things. Those born in December must beware of indecision, the influence of Sagittarius is upon them and its faults do not amalgamate well with those of their own sign. Therefore all Capricorn people should cultivate some ambition—let them fix their eyes on a star and they will climb towards it. Without the guiding light they may wander here and there without meeting success.

These people take life seriously, often a sense of humour is lacking, but they are absolutely true to any trust reposed in them. All the occult, all the hidden mysteries of science appeal strongly. They will be happy in any such research work, but above all else any career connected with agriculture, mining, or building will be congenial, or they should find work in some large public institution.

It is difficult for Capricorn people to say what is in their hearts. They will brood over a slight or injury, while the person with whom they are offended wonders what is the matter. Let them make up their minds to speak out, and a grave defect of their nature will be conquered.

As a rule it is better for them not to marry too early. They will find their best chance of happy comradeship with the people of Taurus—naturally the bull and the goat have much in common—Cancer and Virgo, or under their own sign. Saturday is their day, eight is their number, their jewels are the ruby, the black onyx and the malachite, while jet is fortunate to them also, as is coal. Their metal is lead, and their colour dark brown, deep purple or black.

THE HOUSE OF AQUARIUS, THE WATER BEARER

The sun enters this House approximately on January 20th and stays till February 19th. Saturn is the ruling planet according to the old astrologers, but modern teachers give Uranius, a planet which was not discovered until recent times, though its existence was suspected.

Old Zodiacs show the symbol of this house as a pitcher of water, and we can understand the reason when we remember the downpour of rain which visits most of Europe during this period. "February fill dyke," as the countryfolk say, is more than justified as a name. Thus the Chaldeans called this sign the Watering Pot, the Chinese The Vase Full, the Arabians the Pitcher, the Greeks the Water Pourer, for they added the figure of a man, showing him with the vase of water on his shoulder.

Aquarius people are perhaps the most attractive of all, generally exercising great fascination which brings them hosts of friends. They enjoy company because they are interested in their fellow men and love to take part in any gathering for education or amusement. The drama, art, and literature appeal to them, and they follow public affairs closely. Generally they have the uncanny gift of reading what is in the minds of those around, and have a curious power of soothing and influencing the mentally afflicted.

As a rule Aquarius people are apart from the commonplace and their lives are out of the ordinary also. They have many changes of fortune, but meet them with patience and courage; they are faithful and reliable in all things. On the other hand, let them beware of a tendency to become discontented, to be for ever envying others better off than themselves, and to dwell on personal grievances. Generally they will worry over money matters but quite often this is a sign of their better nature, because they will fret for the sake of others, not of themselves. When they have money they give it lavishly, yet are apt to be cheese-paring in small economies. Those born during the first part of the sign are more easily led and not so reliable as the others. Those of the later period, when the influence of Mercury is being felt, will turn to acting or art or literature or to some employment that is for public good.

Love making does not come easily to these people, because they are extremely sensitive and seldom show what they feel, yet they are true as steel, and when their love is once given it is for all time. They will find themselves most in sympathy with those born under their own sign, or under Gemini or Libra. Other favourable periods for the birth dates of their friends would be Leo and Scorpio.

8 is their number, and their colours should be dark as those of Capricorn, while their jewels are the garnet and the zircon. Saturday is their day, and they will find any work connected with lead or coal will be particularly fortunate.

THE HOUSE OF PISCES, THE FISHES

The sun enters this House on February 19th and leaves it on March 20th. Ruling planet Jupiter.

Greek mythology tells us the two fishes represented here are Venus and Cupid, who were walking on the banks of the river Euphrates when they were attacked by Typhon, and in order to escape from the very unpleasant monster, Venus changed herself and her son into fish. Plainly it is another form of the Pan legend told in the account of Capricorn.

The symbol of the House is two fishes swimming different ways, and Pisces people are curiously dual in their characters, which often makes others accuse them of weakness or indecision, though these are not faults of the sign. It is rather because they have so strong a sense of duty towards others that these people are forced by one side of their character to take a course opposed to the judgment of their other side. They are remarkably adaptable, they can settle down in almost any surroundings, they can become popular in almost any society, but are easily influenced by their surroundings. Always they are intensely peace loving, sympathetic, and emotional.

That article on astrology which has been quoted earlier shall be quoted again here. Regarding the people of Pisces it says :—

"Their ability to acquire knowledge is often extraordinary, they seem to learn without the slightest effort, and their memories are remarkable. As children they are usually precocious, and all their lives they are full of interest in all that goes on around them and very observant, with an uncanny gift of being able to understand things without being told.

"Under wrong or suffering they are very patient, yet they worry in secret and suffer greatly from despondency when they cannot see their way clear before them. They are naturally proud and independent, and have a dread of being a trouble to others. . . . There is a love of beauty in their natures, and many artists are born under this sign. They are good mimics, and often succeed on the stage, but often they fail to make the best of themselves because their retiring natures keep them in the background while others with less ability and more conceit thrust themselves forward.

"They are sensitive and impressionable, and can only do their best work when they have sympathy and encouragement. Though they can be easily persuaded and give way to those they love they can be obstinate if anything like tyranny is shown to them. Pisces people often win fame as novelists, they have strong imaginations and romance is born in them. . . . There are strong leanings towards spiritualism in this sign. . . . They generally travel a great deal and voyages are favourable to them. All work and professions connected with the sea will attract them. It is the sign of the sailor and the lover of adventure. . . . All business in which liquids are bought and sold or manufactured will bring them good luck, but it is specially necessary for Pisces people to be on their guard against habits of intemperance or the taking of narcotics. These often cause trouble to them, although it may not be from their own failings but the faults of others.

" Living as they do in their feelings and emotions their health depends on their minds to a great extent. They need tranquility and restful surroundings. Sea air is always beneficial to them. Like those born under Cancer and Scorpio they should try to get to the sea when they are ill, and the complaints to which they are most subject are those which sea voyages have often cured when all other means have failed.

" Those who claim Pisces as their birth sign are amongst the most hospitable of beings. If they are well off they will keep open house, if they are poor they are ready to share the last crust. Love of animals is another feature of the sign. In fact all that is helpless and unable to take its own part makes a strong appeal to them. They are tender-hearted to a fault, and thus easily imposed upon—though often they realise they are helping an undesirable—another proof of their dual nature."

The people with whom they are most likely to find happiness are those of Cancer, Scorpio, or their own sign, and in a lesser degree with the people of Taurus and Capricorn. Their number is 3, though 4 and 7 will have strong influences over them; their day is Thursday; their colour purple; their stone the amethyst; while their special talisman is the swastika, the hammer of Thor.

THE END